Multi-Use
COLLAPSIBLE
BASKET PATTERNS

by Rick and Karen Longabaugh

Fox Chapel Publishing Company Inc.

1970 Broad Street
East Petersburg, PA 17520
www.scrollsawer.com

Dedication

We dedicate this book to our two sons, James and Cameron, and to our families for all the unending faith and support they have shown us.

Acknowledgements / Credits

Pattern Designs

Rick Longabaugh
Ardis Longabaugh
Tana Althauser
Lorna Smith

Graphic Design

Lorna Smith Graphic Design
Chehalis, Washington

Photography

Greg Krogstad Photography
Seattle, Washington

©Copyright 1992, 1997 by Rick and Karen Longabaugh,
THE BERRY BASKET. Printed in the United States
ISBN # 1-56523-088-4

To order your copy of this book,
please send check or money order
for $12.95 plus $3 postage to:
Fox Chapel Book Orders
1970 Broad Street
East Petersburg, PA 17520

Try your favorite book supplier first!

Contents

Instructions

Introduction

All the patterns in this book are designed to be cut on the scrollsaw. We have titled this book *MULTI-USE COLLAPSIBLE BASKET PATTERNS* because of their versatility. The majority of patterns are designed to be used as either a basket, clock, mirror, picture frame, or weather station. **It's like getting 5 books for the price of 1!**

Materials

Scrollsaw blades - #7 to cut the pattern and
    #9 to cut the basket rungs
3/4 " Hardwood (see page 5)
Spray adhesive
Oil (Min-Wax, Danish or Tung)
Drill bits - 1/16" and 1/8"

Countersink - 1/4" to 3/8"
Router bit - 1/4" roundover
Small drum or pad sander
6/32 Machine screws: flathead or
    roundhead
or #6 Wood screws: flathead or
    roundhead

General Instructions

To use this pattern book most effectively, we suggest making photo copies of the patterns you wish to cut out. An advantage to the copier is that you can enlarge or reduce the pattern to fit the size wood you choose to use. Use a spray adhesive to adhere the pattern to the wood. Spray adhesives can be purchased at most arts & crafts, photography, and department stores. Pay special attention to purchase one that states "temporary bond" or "repositionable". Lightly spray the back of the pattern, not the wood, then position the pattern onto the work piece.

Two factors will determine how deep the basket will fold out, the thickness of the blade, and the bevel of the table when cutting. A thicker blade produces a deeper basket, as does the 4° bevel over the 5°. Therefore, we recommend practicing with an inexpensive grade of wood until you determine the proper bevel for the thickness of the blade you are using. In the materials listed above we have recommended 2 different scrollsaw blade sizes. We suggest using the #7 blade to cut the pattern with, and the #9 blade to cut the basket rungs. The following chart gives the approximate bevels for most #9 blades. However keep in mind that different brands of blades will vary in thickness, which will then affect how deep the basket will fold out. To determine the bevels in the chart below, a #9 blade with the following specs was used: width .053, thickness .018 and TPI 11.5.

To measure the circle, oval or heart measure at the basket's pivot points from one dotted line on the pattern to the other (see example at right). Find the size of the circle, oval, or heart (to the nearest 1/2") on the chart below to give you the proper bevel. Keep in mind that if you reduce or enlarge the pattern you will need to adjust the bevel accordingly.

Bevel Chart

Circle	4 1/2"	5"	5 1/2"	6"	6 1/2"	7"
bevel	6°	5 1/2°	5°	4 1/2°	4°	3 1/2°
Oval	5"	5 1/2"	6"	6 1/2"	7"	7 1/2"
bevel	7°	6 1/2°	6°	5 1/2°	5 °	4 1/2°
Standing Heart	4 1/2"	5"	5 1/2"	6"	6 1/2"	7"
bevel	6°	5 1/2°	5°	4 1/2°	4°	3 1/2°
Side Heart	4 1/2"	5"	5 1/2"	6"	6 1/2"	7"
bevel	6°	5 1/2°	5°	4 1/2°	4°	3 1/2°

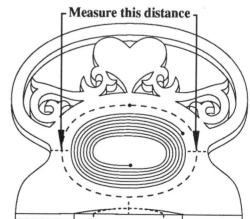

Measure this distance

General Instructions (continued)

The baskets pictured in this book have been cut out of the following hardwoods: ash, maple - curly and birdseye, walnut - eastern and curly, flaming birch, mahogany - cuban and ribbon, curly hickory, curly cherry, and red oak. Please keep in mind, however, that this is not a complete list of the beautiful hardwoods available.

We have stated a drill bit size and corresponding screw size in the materials listed above. If, however, you choose to use a size other than what is listed, use a drill bit one size smaller than the screws you are using. This will ensure that the screws will fit snugly, providing enough resistance so the basket does not swing freely. You can determine the length of the screw you need for any given pivot point by measuring the length of its dotted line on the pattern. If you wish to counter sink the screw, keep in mind that you will need a shorter length of screw than what the dotted line measured.

Sand any rough edges on the outer shape and the first rung of the basket. If the basket or foot catches on any edges when pivoted, try sanding a little more. For a more refined look use a 1/4" roundover router bit on the edges.

When the basket is completed, soak it in oil according to the manufactures' instructions.

Helpful Hints

Round / Oval / Heart baskets - If you have trouble getting the basket to fold out completely (see figure 1a), you may need to adjust your bevel. If you previously used a 6° bevel, try using a 5° or 4°, if you used a 7° bevel, try a 6° or 5°, etc. This will allow the basket to fold out deeper (see figure 1b). If the opposite is happening and the basket rungs are too loose, again you will need to adjust the bevel. If you used a 6° bevel, try a 7° or 8°, if you used a 7° bevel, try an 8° or 9°, etc.

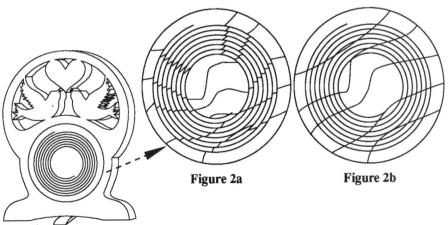

Figure 1a

Figure 1b

Round Baskets - Occasionally the basket will not fold out completely even if the proper bevel was used. Due to the complexity of the grain patterns in some woods, the basket will turn so that the grain does not align after you have cut the basket rungs (see figure 2a). If so, realign the grain by turning the basket rungs clockwise or counter clockwise (see figure 2b), and open the basket.

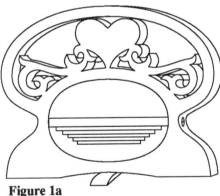

Figure 2a

Figure 2b

1

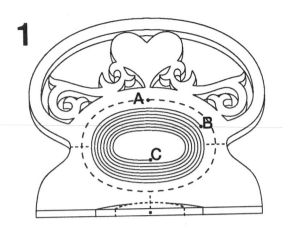

Basket Instructions

Step 1 Adhere pattern to work piece. Cut outer shape and design of basket.

Step 2 Mark the drill points using a hammer and center punch. Drill and countersink basket and foot pivot points the length of their dashed lines using a 1/8" drill bit and a 1/4" to 3/8" countersink.

2

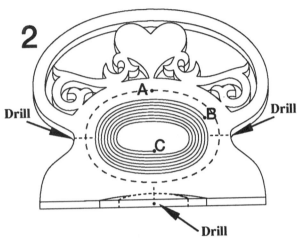

Drill   Drill

Drill

Step 3 With table flat, cut along dashed lines to separate foot. Drill at points A, B and C using a 1/16" drill bit. Beginning at point A, cut along dashed line (with table flat) to separate inner basket from the outer shape.

Step 4 After measuring the size of the circle, oval, or heart basket to be cut out please refer to the chart on page 4 for the proper bevel. Using the bevel indicated, cut the basket rungs following the solid line. If your table tilts to the left begin your cut at point C and finish at point B. If your table tilts to the right begin your cut at point B and finish at point C. **Note:** It is easier to begin at point C and end at point B.

3

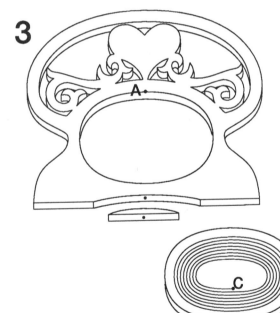

Step 5 Using the 1/4" roundover bit, rout where indicated on the example below. Sand where needed. Assemble basket and foot with screws at drilled pivot points. Soak in oil according to manufacturer's instructions.

Rout

5

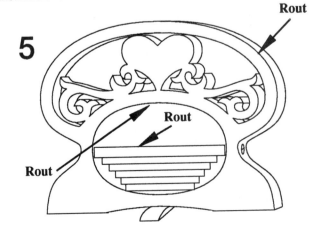

Rout

Rout

4

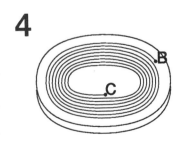

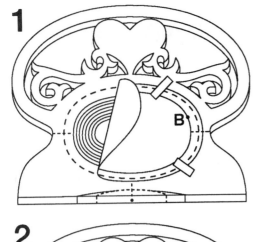

1

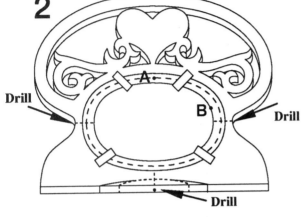

2

Drill

Drill

Drill

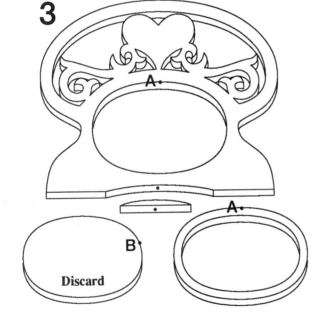

3

Discard

Mirror/Picture Frame Instructions

To begin, choose the mirror/picture frame from pages 9-11 that matches the pattern you wish to make. Use scissors to cut the paper frame pattern slightly larger than the outer dashed lines. Align the dashed pivot point lines on the mirror/picture frame pattern with those on the basket pattern. Use a spray adhesive or tape to adhere in place.

Step 1 Adhere pattern to work piece. Cut outer shape and design.

Step 2 Mark the drill points using a hammer and center punch. Drill and countersink mirror/picture frame and foot pivot points the length of their dashed lines using a 1/8" drill bit and 1/4" to 3/8" countersink.

Step 3 With table flat, cut along dashed lines to separate foot. Drill at point A and B using a 1/16" drill bit. Beginning at point A, cut along dashed line to separate mirror/picture frame from outer shape. Then beginning at point B, cut along solid line and discard center piece.

Step 4 Using a 1/4" roundover bit, rout the inner and outer edges of the mirror/picture frame as indicated on the example. Turn the frame over and use a 1/4" rabbetting bit on the inner edge of the frame, routing 1/4" deep. This will allow you to recess the mirror or picture (glass optional).

Step 5 Using the 1/4" roundover bit, rout where indicated on the example. Sand where needed. Assemble mirror/picture frame and foot with screws at drilled pivot points. Soak in oil according to manufacturer's instructions. Insert mirror or picture into frame. Use a small amount of glue or silicon to hold mirror or picture in place. **Note:** Most retail glass supply stores will cut glass and mirror to the size and shape you need.

4

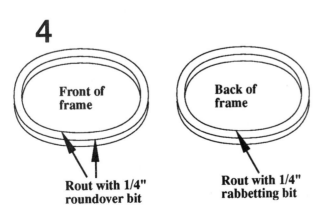

Front of frame

Back of frame

Rout with 1/4" roundover bit

Rout with 1/4" rabbetting bit

Rout

5

Rout

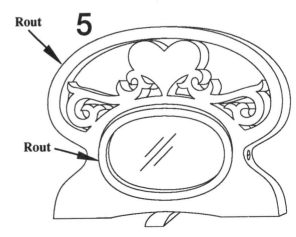

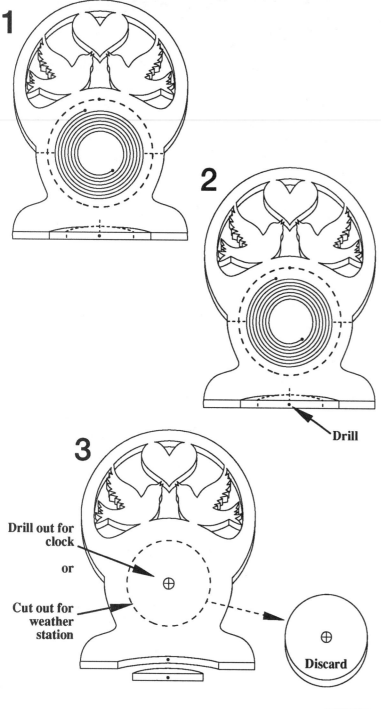

Clock/Weather Station Instructions

Step 1 Adhere pattern to work piece. Cut outer shape and design.

Step 2 Mark the foot drill point using a hammer and center punch. Drill and countersink the foot pivot point the length of the dashed line using a 1/8" drill bit and 1/4" to 3/8" countersink.

Step 3 With table flat, cut along dashed lines to separate foot. **Clock:** Determine the center point of the pattern and mark for drilling. Drill the size of hole needed for the clock's hand shaft according to the manufacturer's instructions. **Weather Station:** Determine the center point of the pattern and mark. Use a compass to draw a circle the size needed to insert the weather station according to the manufacturer's instructions. Cut this circle out and discard.

Step 4 Using a 1/4" roundover bit, rout where indicated on the example. Sand where needed. Assemble foot with screw at drilled pivot point. Soak in oil according to manufacturer's instructions.

Step 5 Assemble clock/weather station according to the manufacturer's instructions.

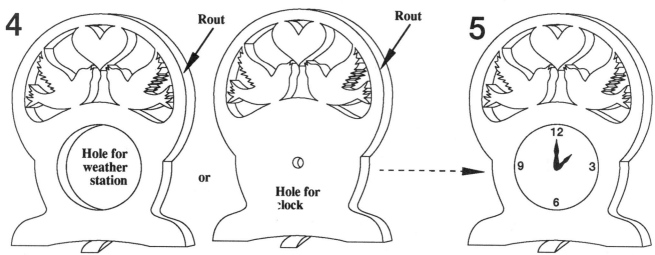

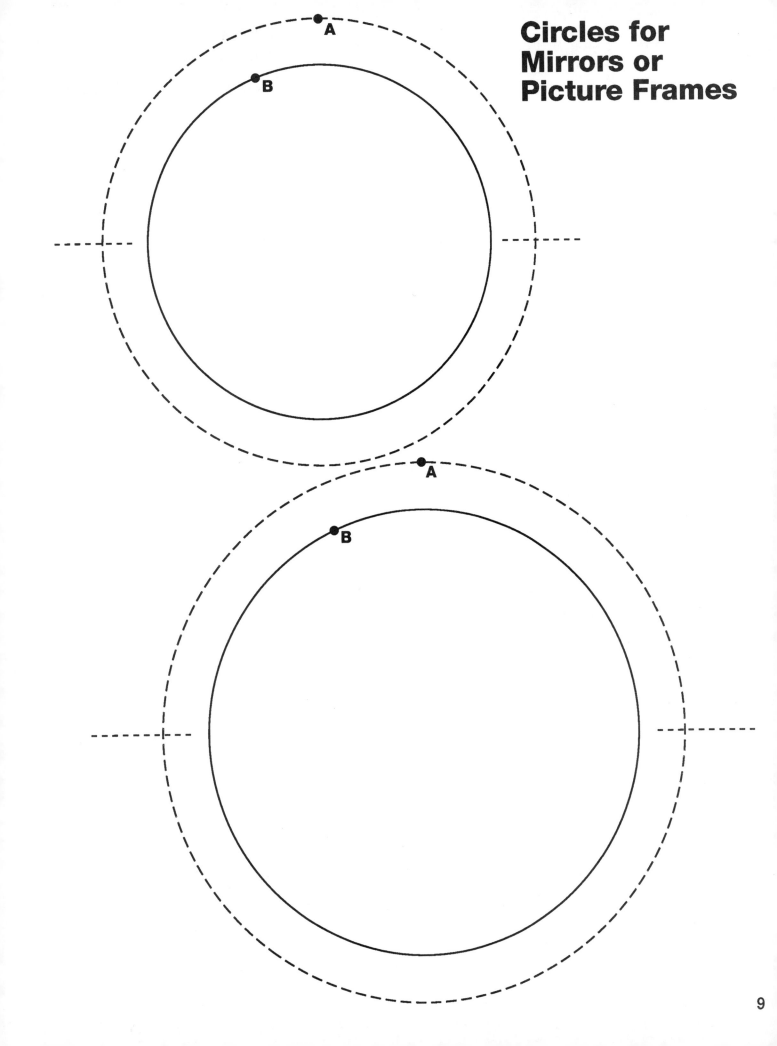

Circles for Mirrors or Picture Frames

9

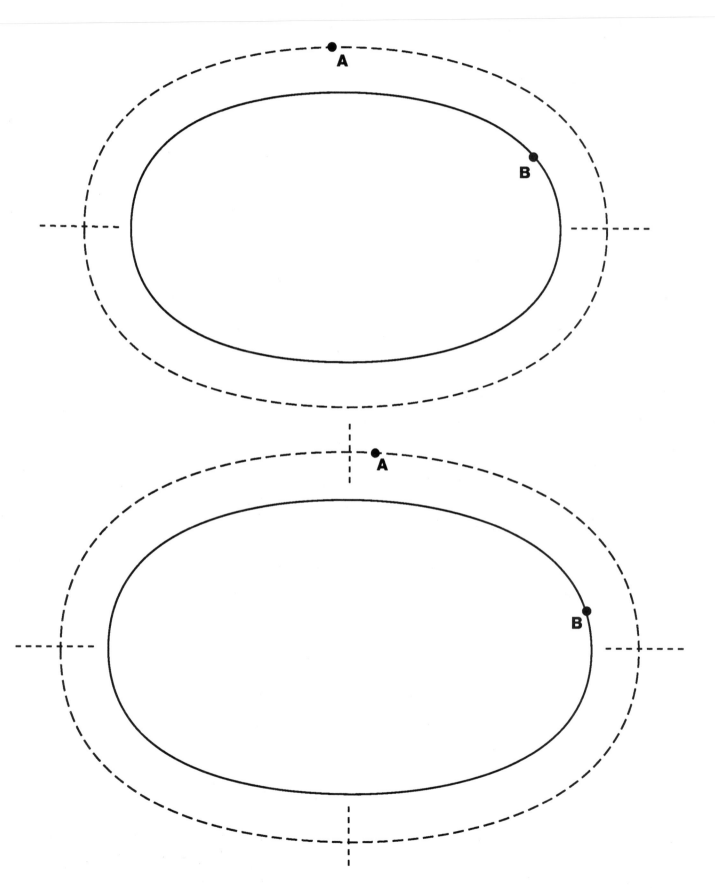

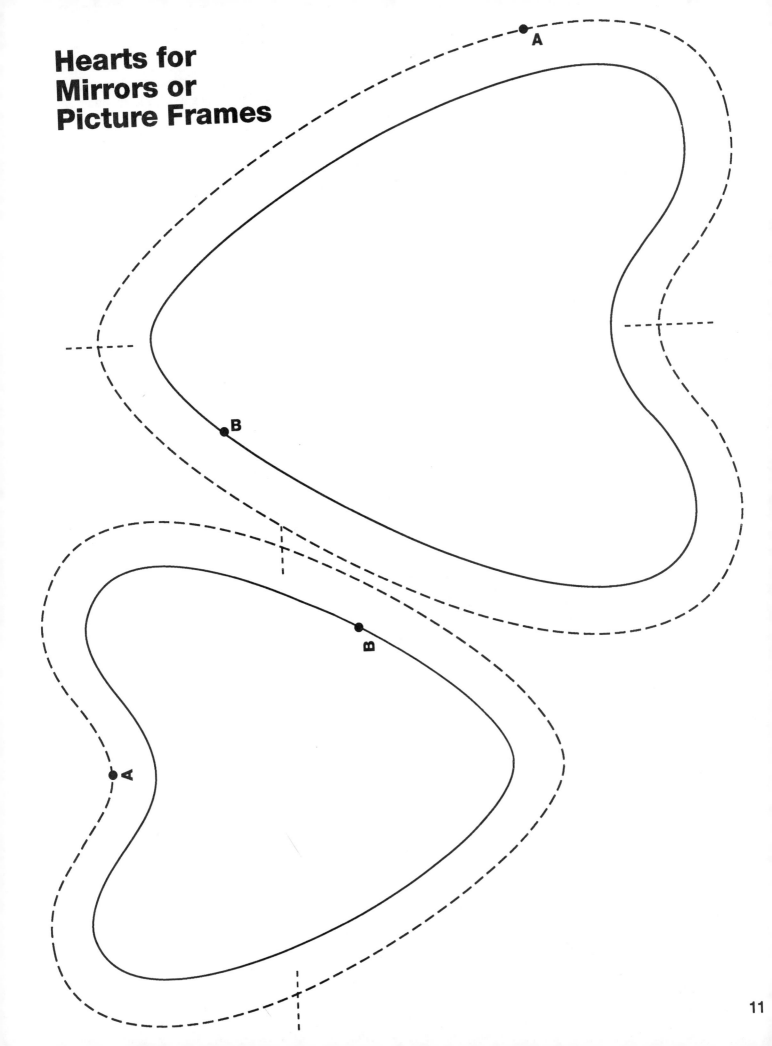

Hearts for Mirrors or Picture Frames

A

B

B

A

11

Numbers

The following numbers can be used with a few of the patterns to customize them for birthdays, anniversaries, or other special occasions. The patterns that allow for this are found on pages 15, 21, 26, and 37. On page 37, the word LUV can be removed and replaced with the numbers of your choice.

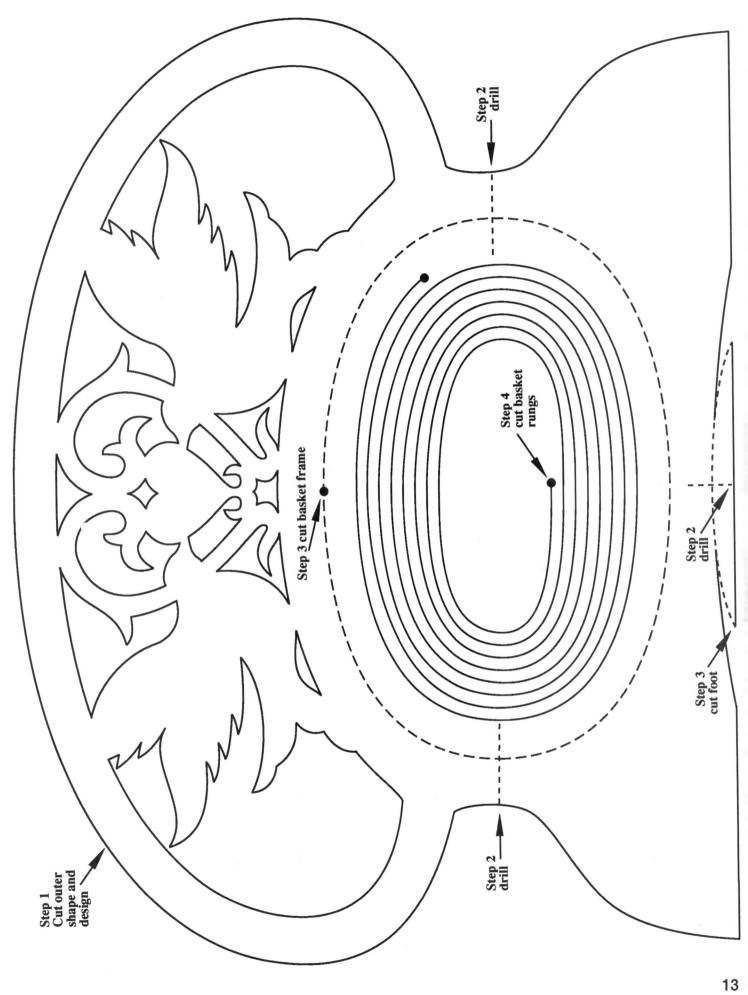

Step 1
Cut outer
shape and
design

Step 2
drill

Step 3 cut basket frame

Step 4
cut basket
rungs

Step 2
drill

Step 2
drill

Step 3
cut foot

13

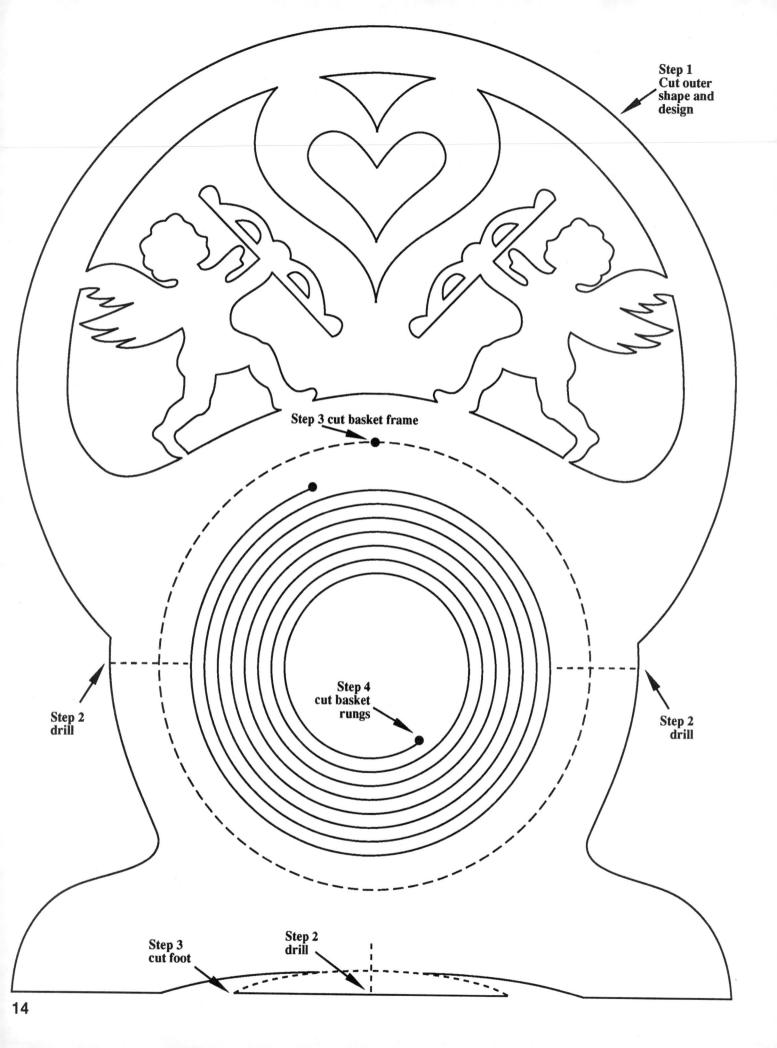

Step 1
Cut outer
shape and
design

Step 3 cut basket frame

Step 2
drill

Step 4
cut basket
rungs

Step 2
drill

Step 3
cut foot

Step 2
drill

14

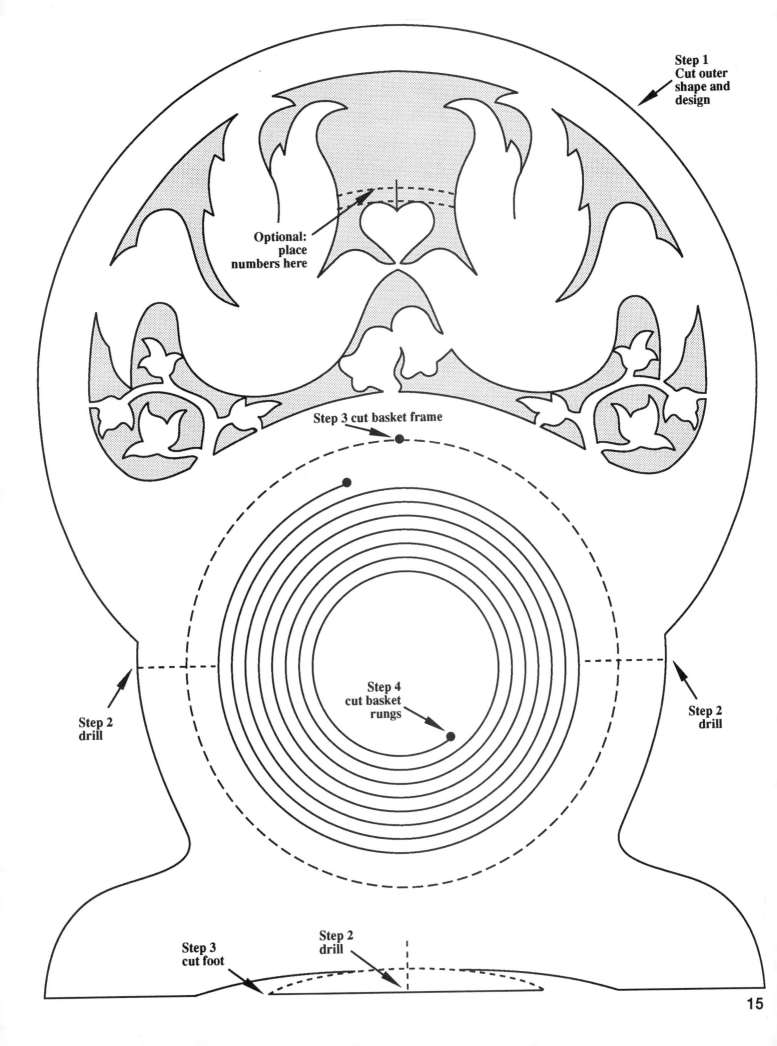

Step 1
Cut outer
shape and
design

Optional:
place
numbers here

Step 3 cut basket frame

Step 2
drill

Step 4
cut basket
rungs

Step 2
drill

Step 3
cut foot

Step 2
drill

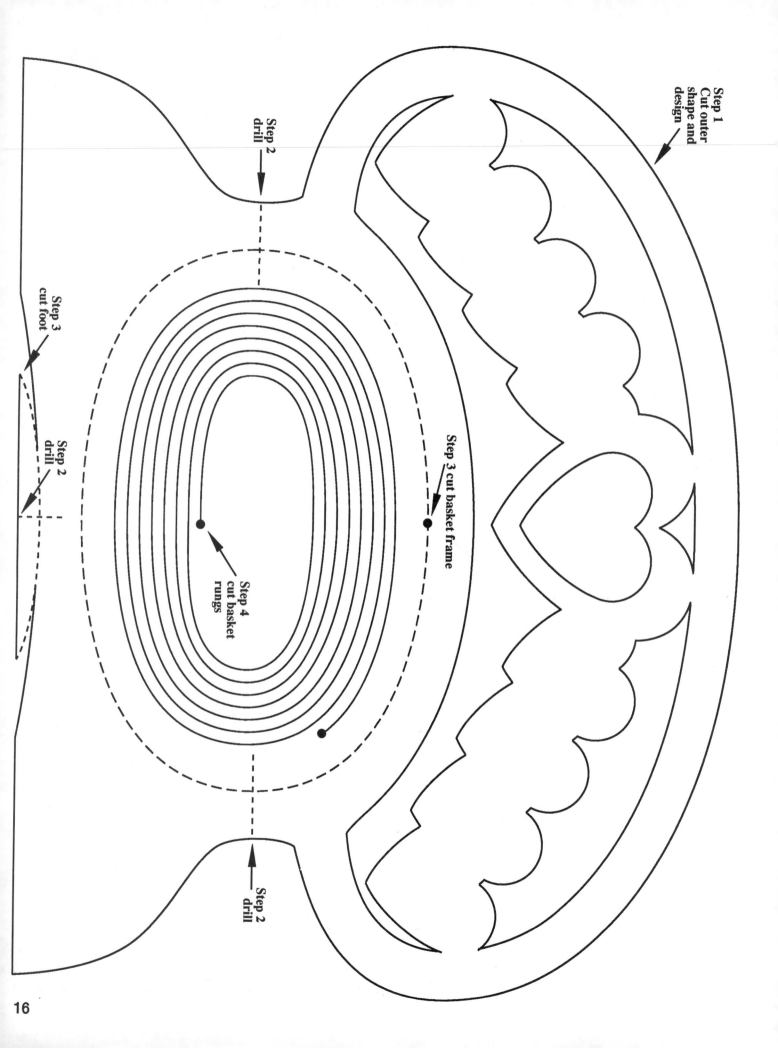

Step 1
Cut outer
shape and
design

Step 2
drill

Step 3
cut foot

Step 2
drill

Step 3 cut basket frame

Step 4
cut basket
rungs

Step 2
drill

Step 2
drill

16

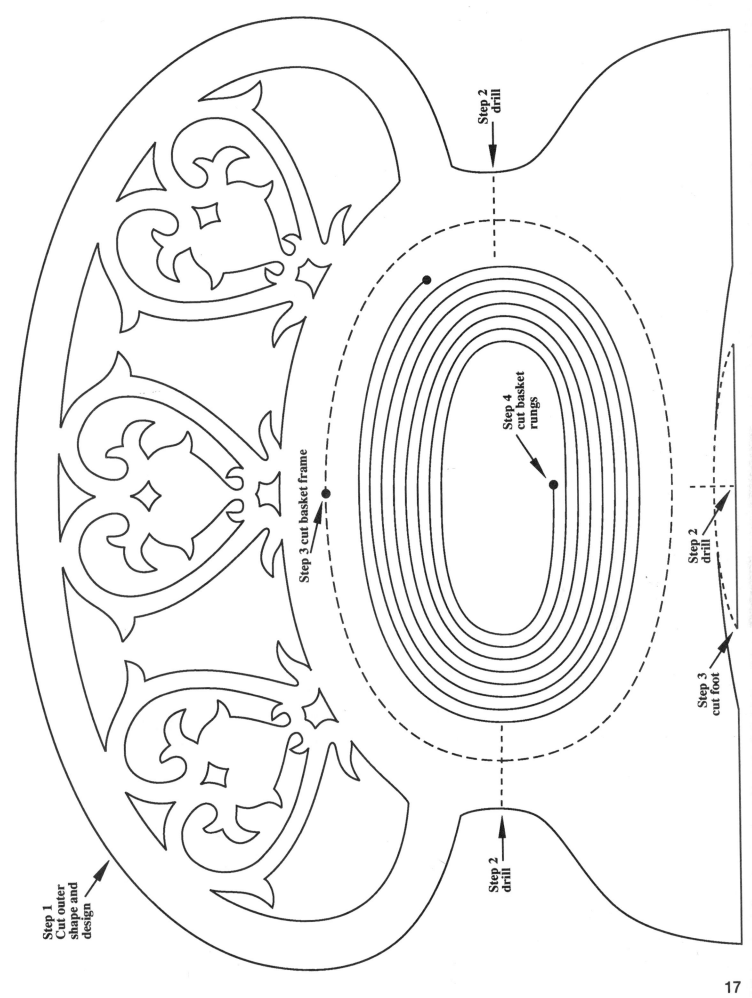

Step 2
drill

Step 3 cut basket frame

Step 4
cut basket
rungs

Step 2
drill

Step 3
cut foot

Step 2
drill

Step 1
Cut outer
shape and
design

17

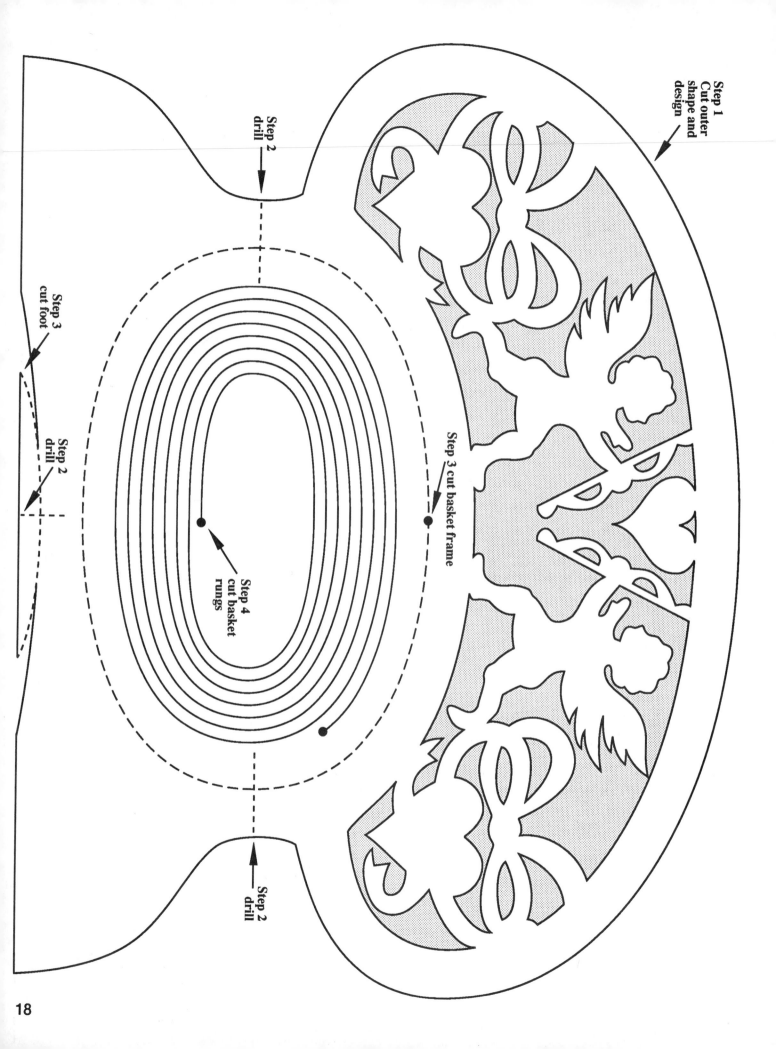

Step 1
Cut outer
shape and
design

Step 2
drill

Step 3
cut foot

Step 2
drill

Step 3 cut basket frame

Step 4
cut basket
rungs

Step 2
drill

18

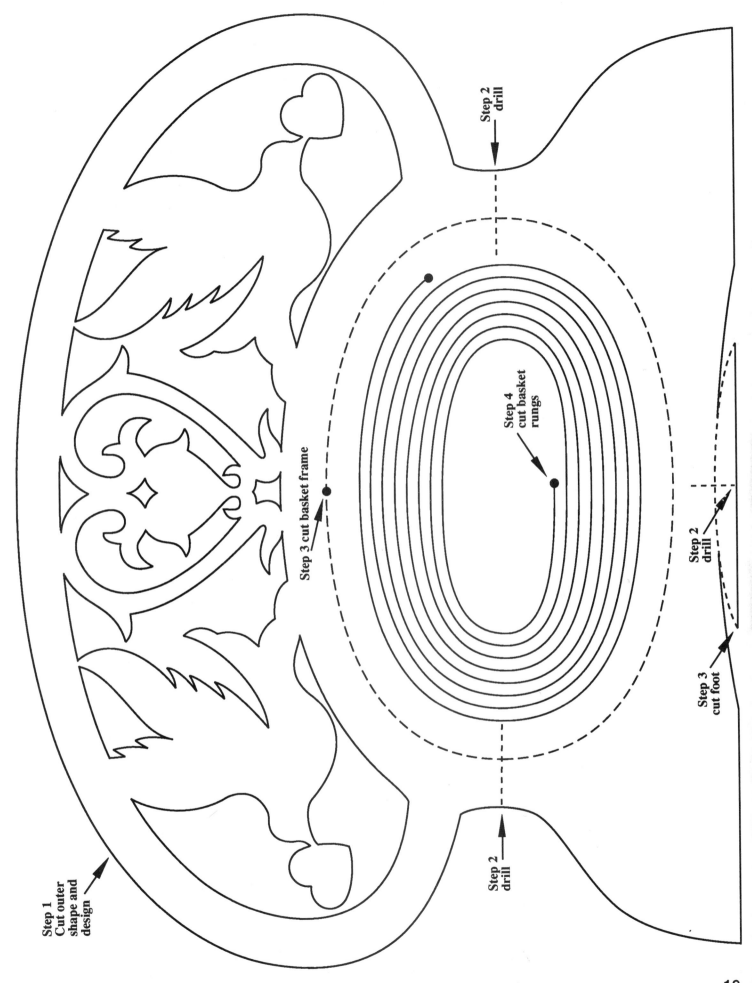

Step 2
drill

Step 3 cut basket frame

Step 4
cut basket
rungs

Step 2
drill

Step 2
drill

Step 3
cut foot

Step 1
Cut outer
shape and
design

19

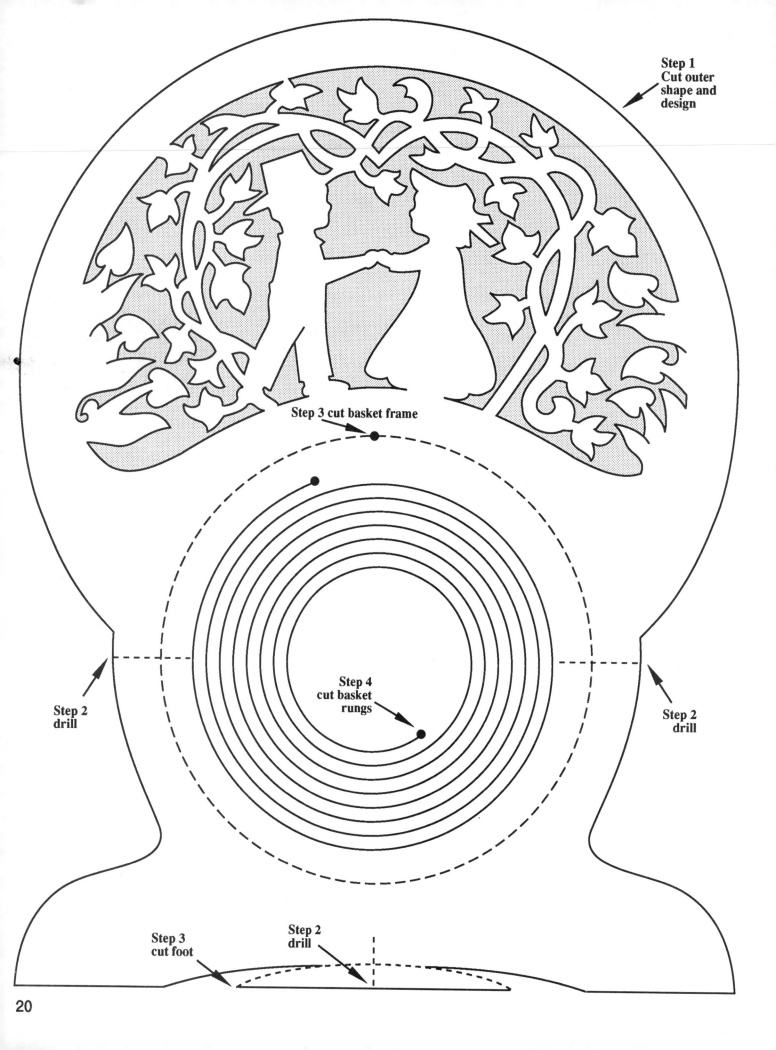

Step 1
Cut outer
shape and
design

Step 3 cut basket frame

Step 2
drill

Step 4
cut basket
rungs

Step 2
drill

Step 3
cut foot

Step 2
drill

20

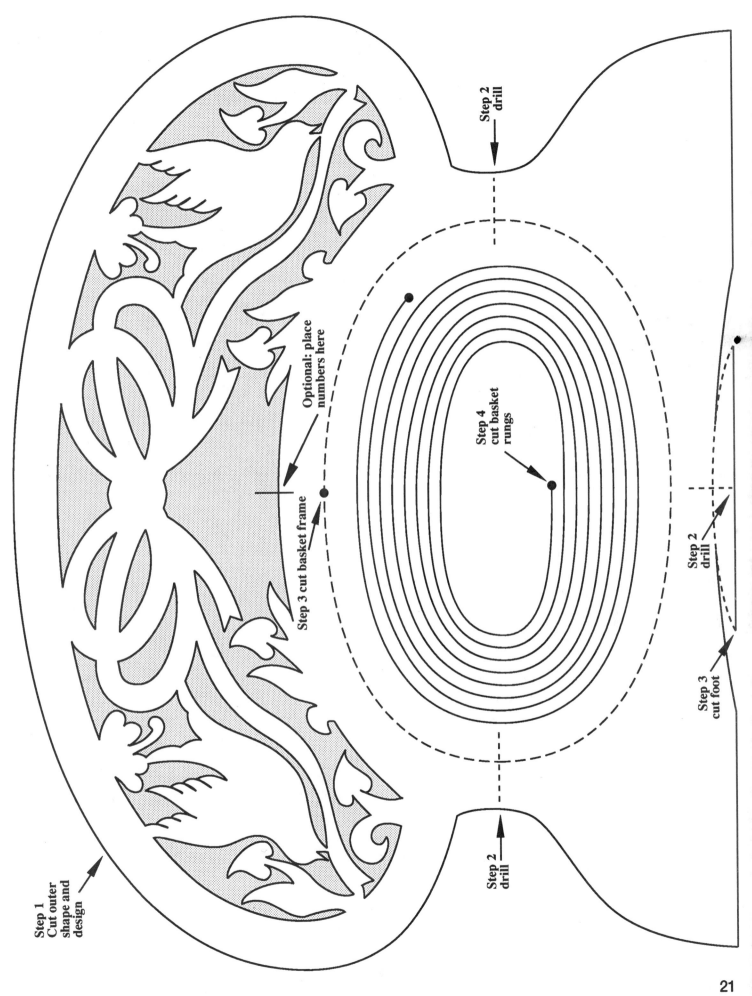

Step 1
Cut outer
shape and
design

Step 3 cut basket frame

Optional: place numbers here

Step 2
drill

Step 4
cut basket
rungs

Step 2
drill

Step 2
drill

Step 3
cut foot

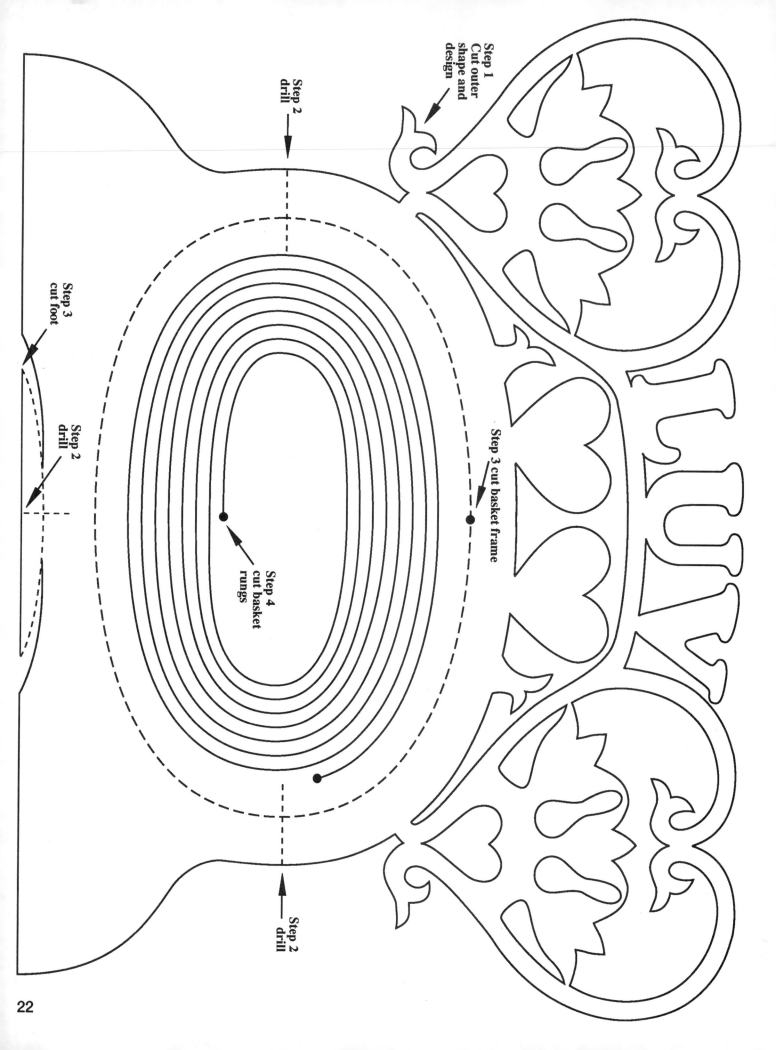

Step 1
Cut outer
shape and
design

Step 2
drill

Step 3
cut foot

Step 2
drill

Step 3 cut basket frame

Step 4
cut basket
rungs

Step 2
drill

22

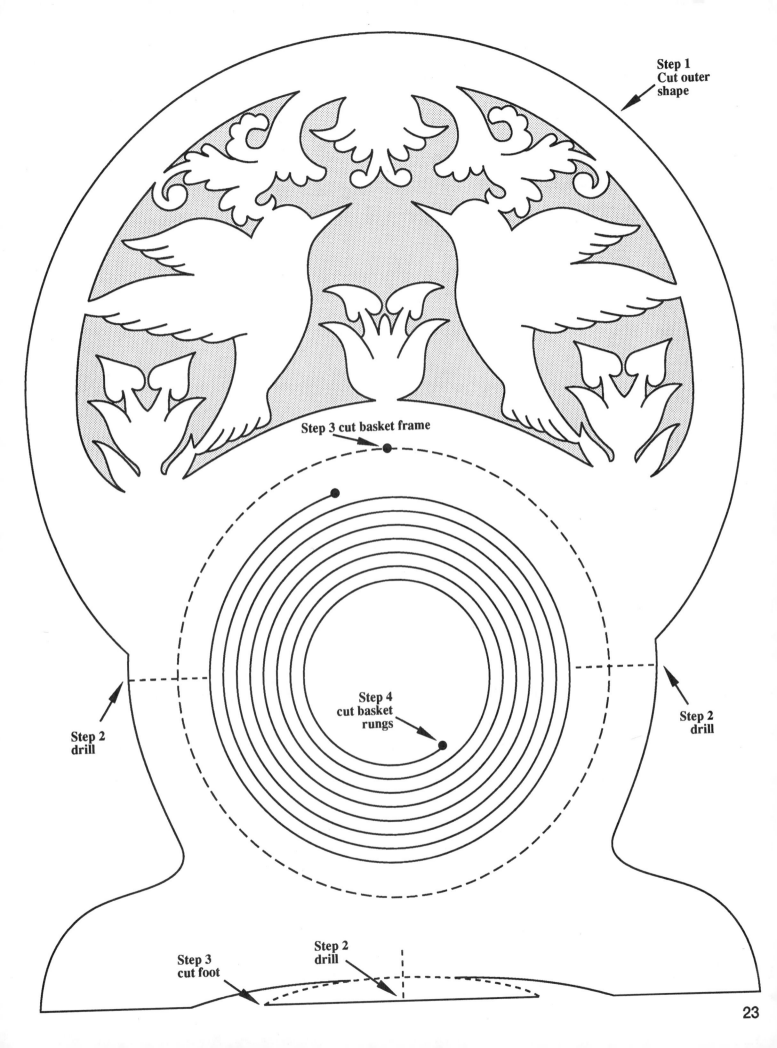

Step 1
Cut outer
shape

Step 3 cut basket frame

Step 2
drill

Step 2
drill

Step 4
cut basket
rungs

Step 3
cut foot

Step 2
drill

23

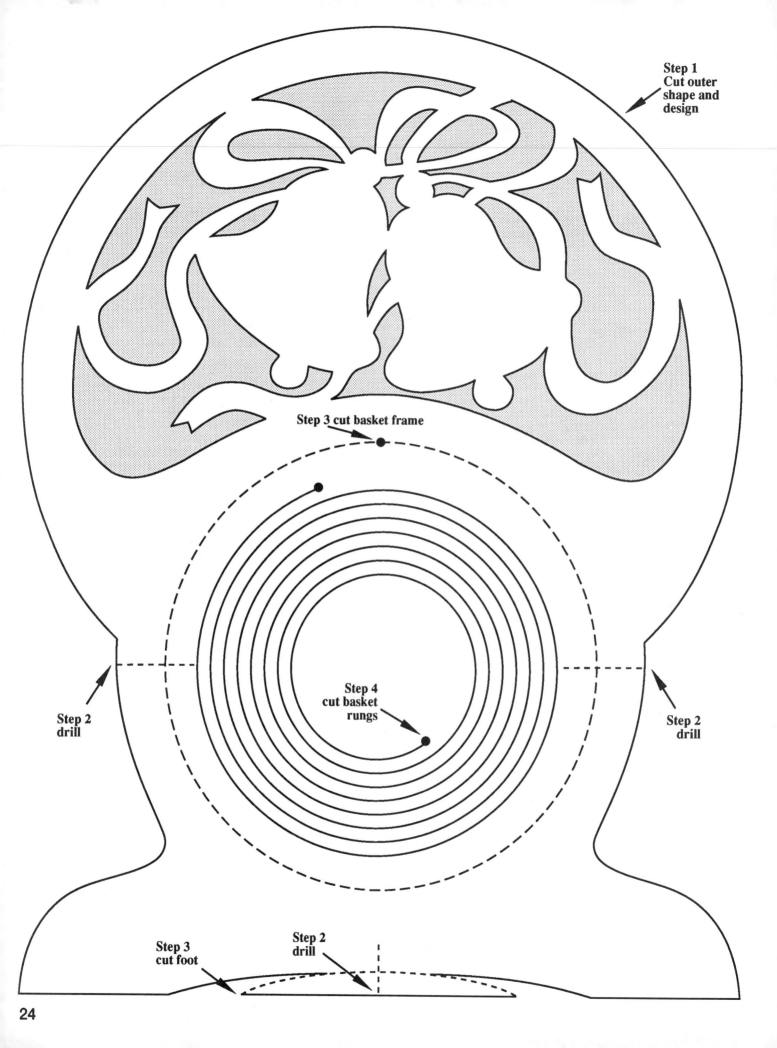

Step 1
Cut outer
shape and
design

Step 3 cut basket frame

Step 2
drill

Step 4
cut basket
rungs

Step 2
drill

Step 3
cut foot

Step 2
drill

24

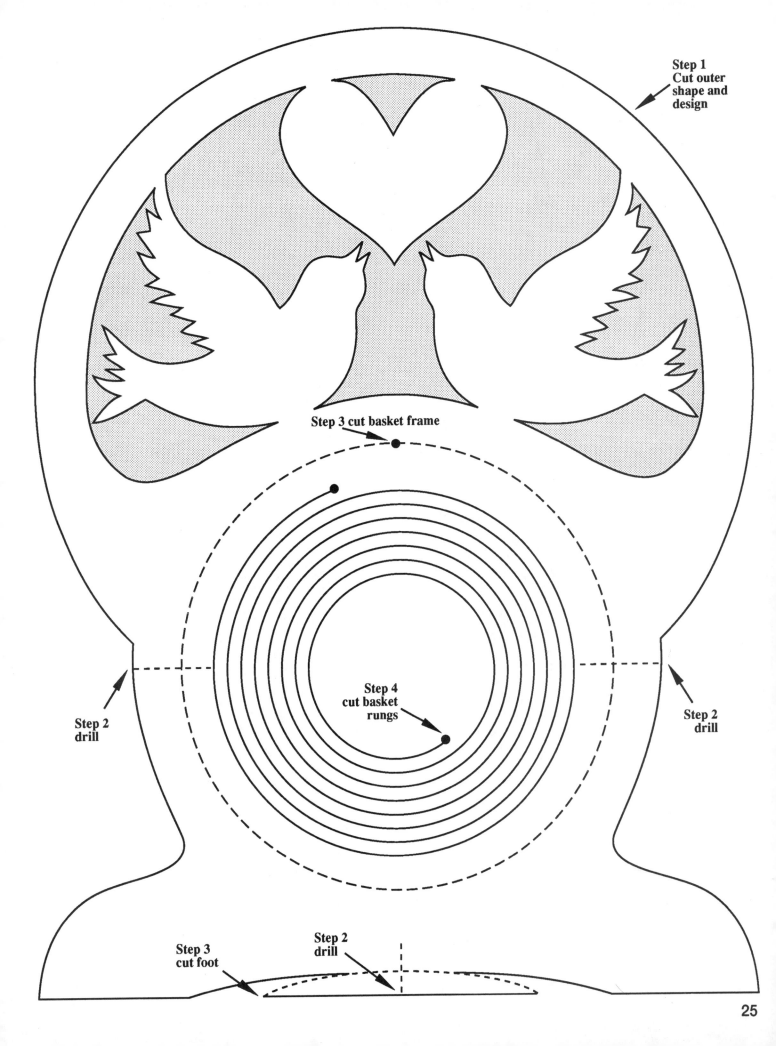

Step 1
Cut outer
shape and
design

Step 3 cut basket frame

Step 4
cut basket
rungs

Step 2
drill

Step 2
drill

Step 3
cut foot

Step 2
drill

25

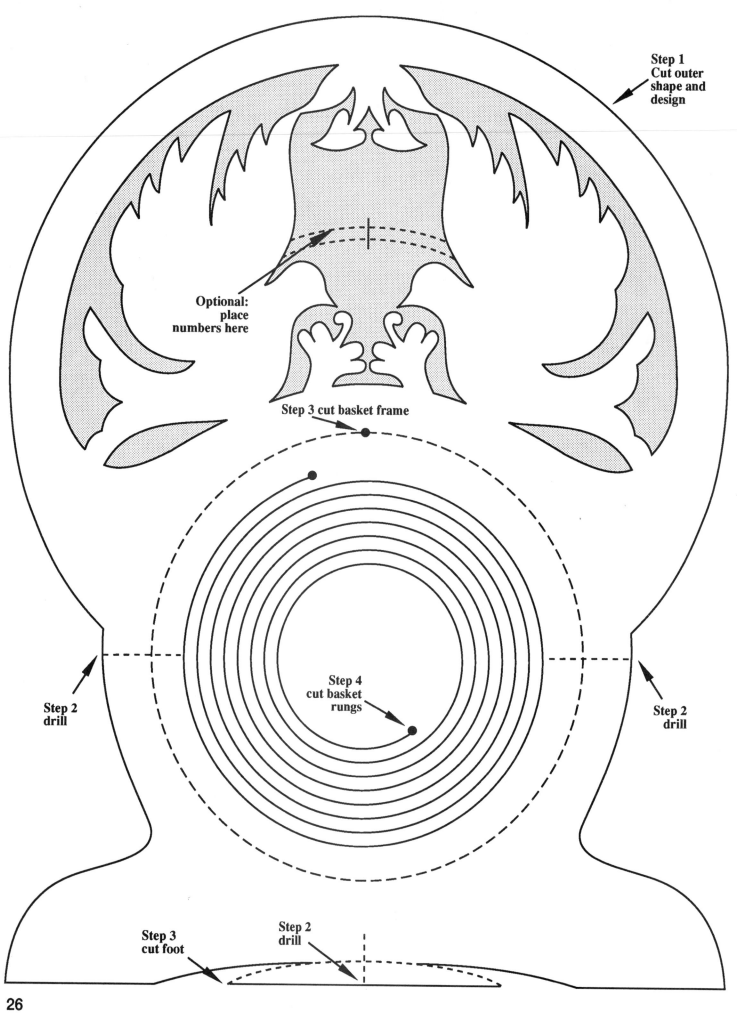

Step 1
Cut outer
shape and
design

Optional:
place
numbers here

Step 3 cut basket frame

Step 2
drill

Step 2
drill

Step 4
cut basket
rungs

Step 3
cut foot

Step 2
drill

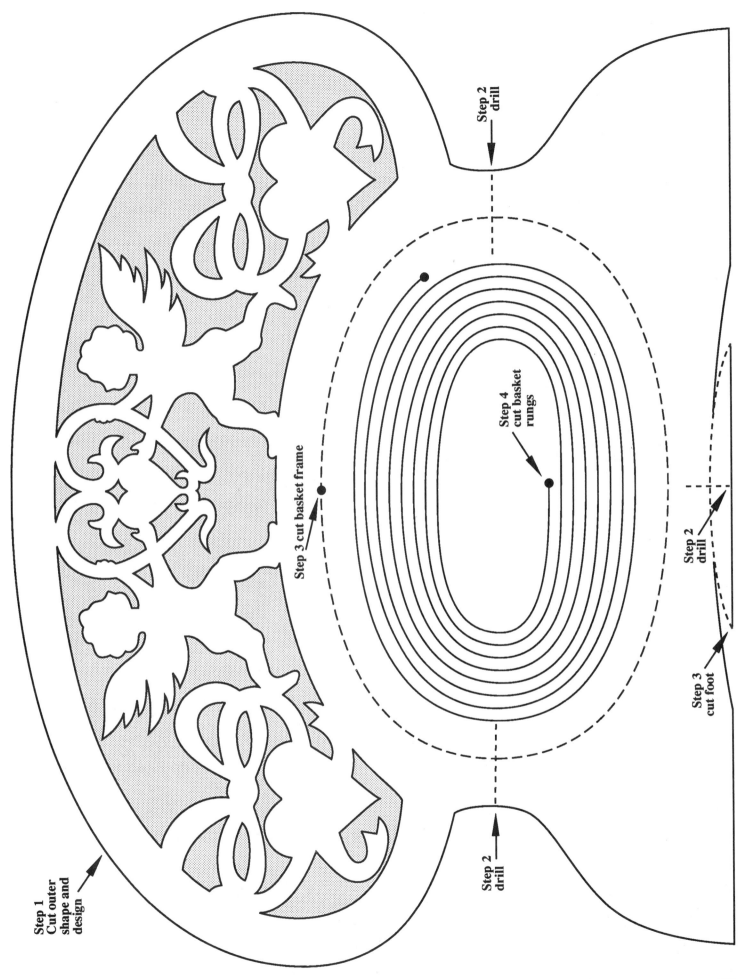

Step 1
Cut outer shape and design

Step 3 cut basket frame

Step 4 cut basket rungs

Step 2 drill

Step 2 drill

Step 2 drill

Step 3 cut foot

27

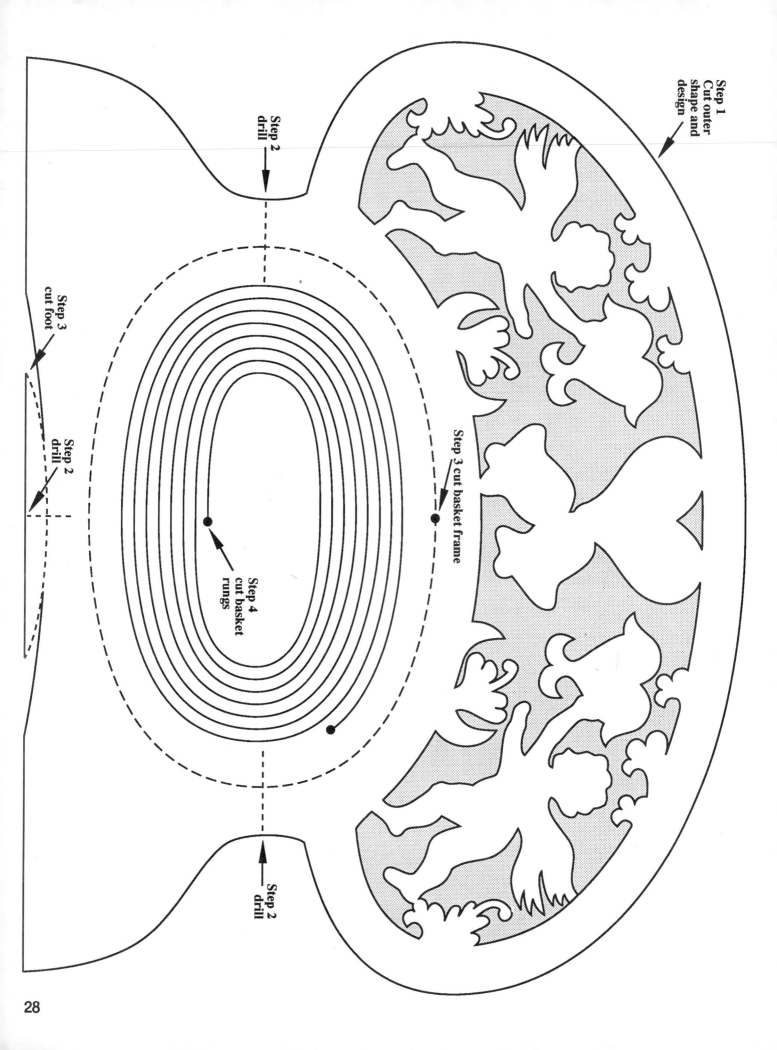

Step 1
Cut outer
shape and
design

Step 2
drill

Step 3
cut foot

Step 2
drill

Step 3 cut basket frame

Step 4
cut basket
rungs

Step 2
drill

28

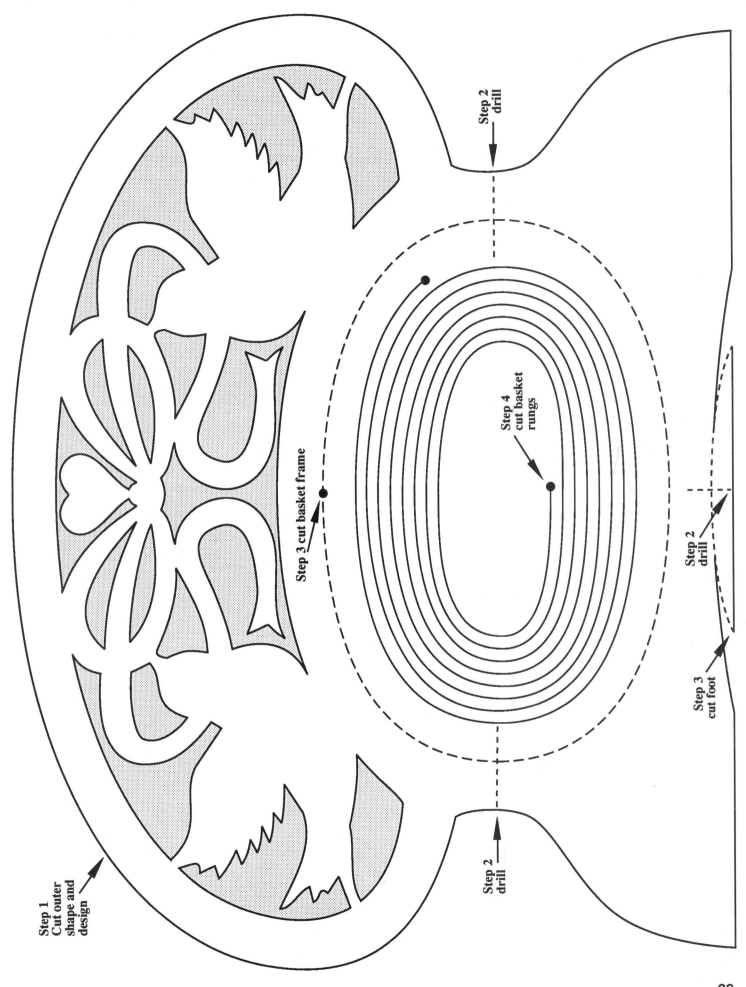

Step 1
Cut outer
shape and
design

Step 2
drill

Step 3 cut basket frame

Step 4
cut basket
rungs

Step 2
drill

Step 2
drill

Step 3
cut foot

Step 2
drill

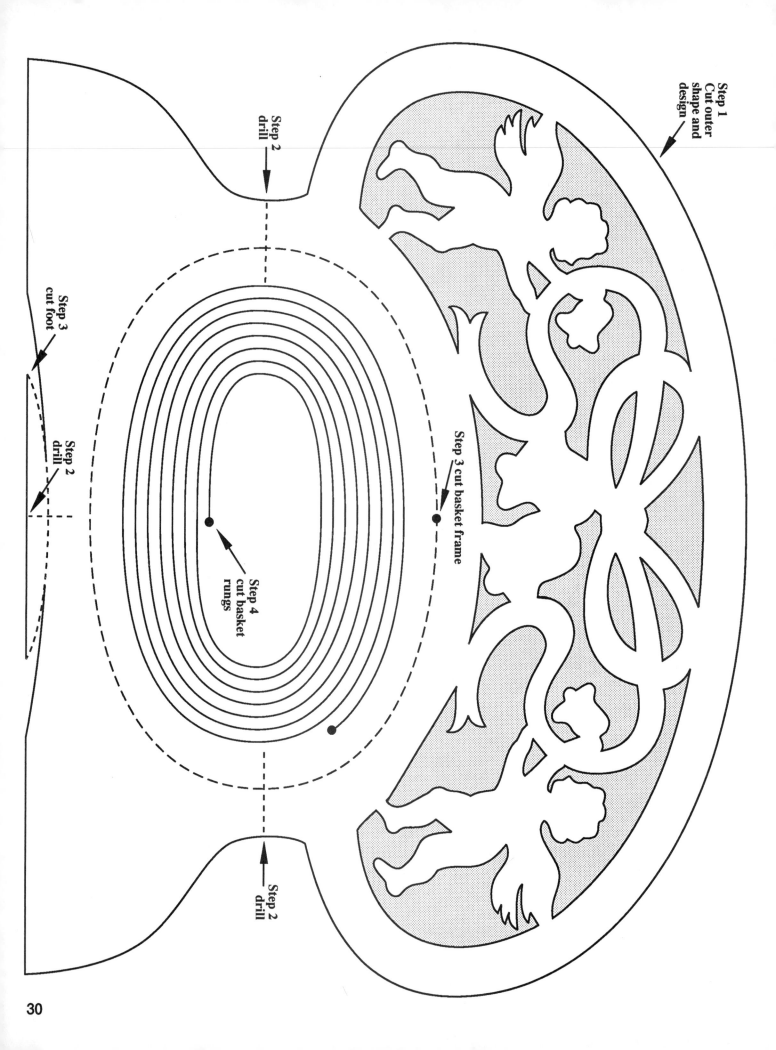

Step 1
Cut outer
shape and
design

Step 2
drill

Step 3
cut foot

Step 2
drill

Step 3 cut basket frame

Step 4
cut basket
rungs

Step 2
drill

Step 2
drill

30

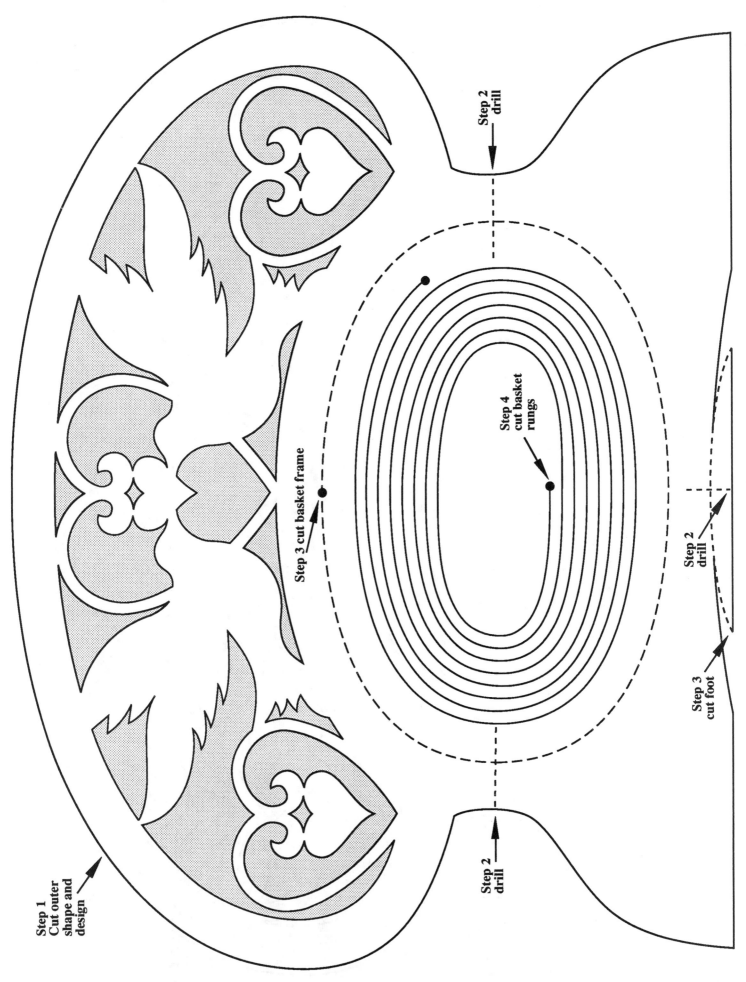

Step 1
Cut outer
shape and
design

Step 2
drill

Step 3 cut basket frame

Step 4
cut basket
rungs

Step 2
drill

Step 3
cut foot

Step 2
drill

Step 2
drill

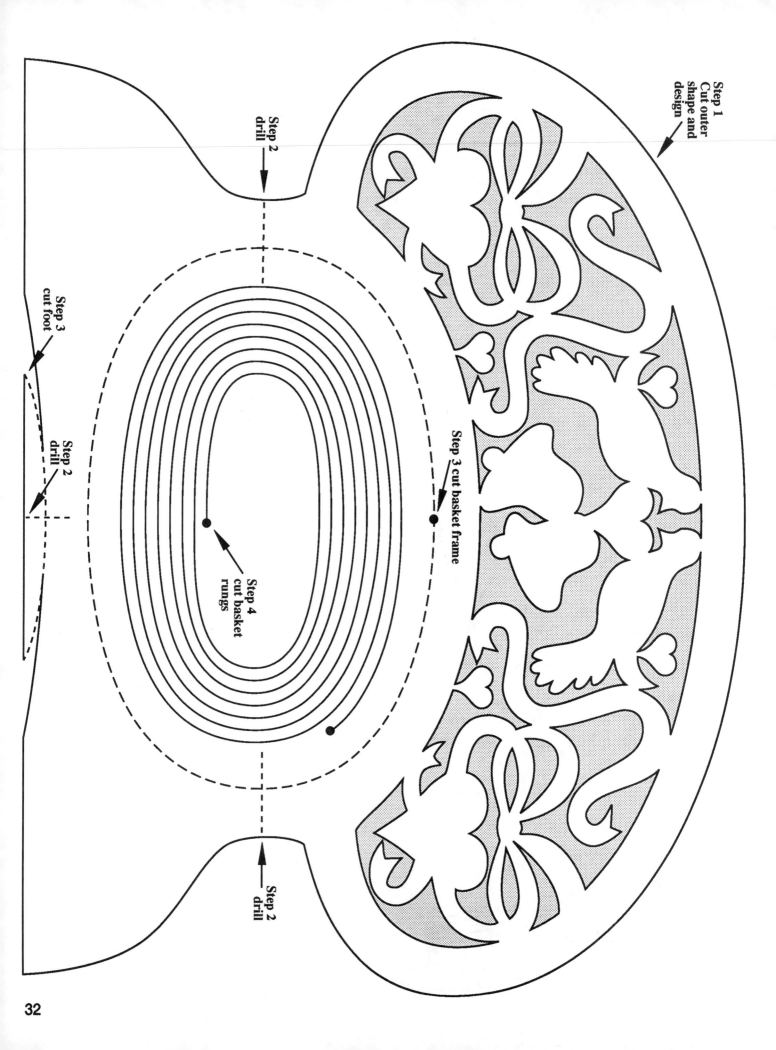

Step 1
Cut outer
shape and
design

Step 2
drill

Step 3
cut foot

Step 2
drill

Step 3 cut basket frame

Step 4
cut basket
rungs

Step 2
drill

Step 2
drill

32

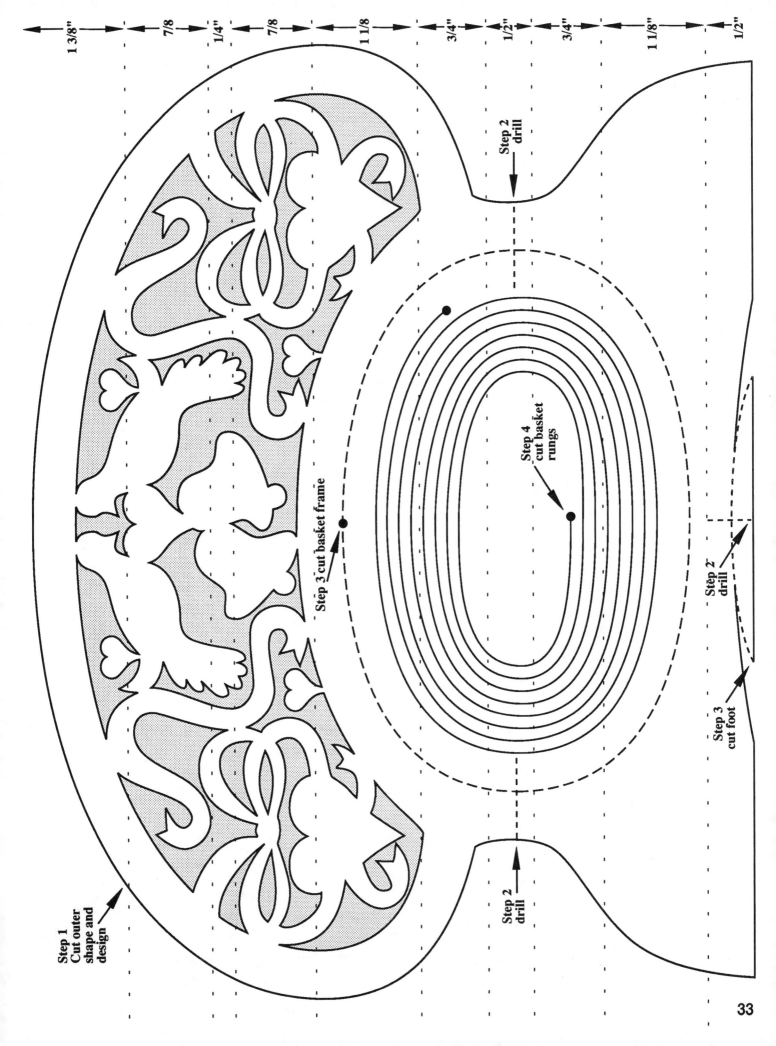

1 3/8"
7/8
1/4"
7/8
1 1/8
3/4"
1/2"
3/4"
1 1/8
1/2"

Step 2
drill

Step 3 cut basket frame

Step 4
cut basket
rungs

Step 2
drill

Step 3
cut foot

Step 2
drill

Step 1
Cut outer
shape and
design

33

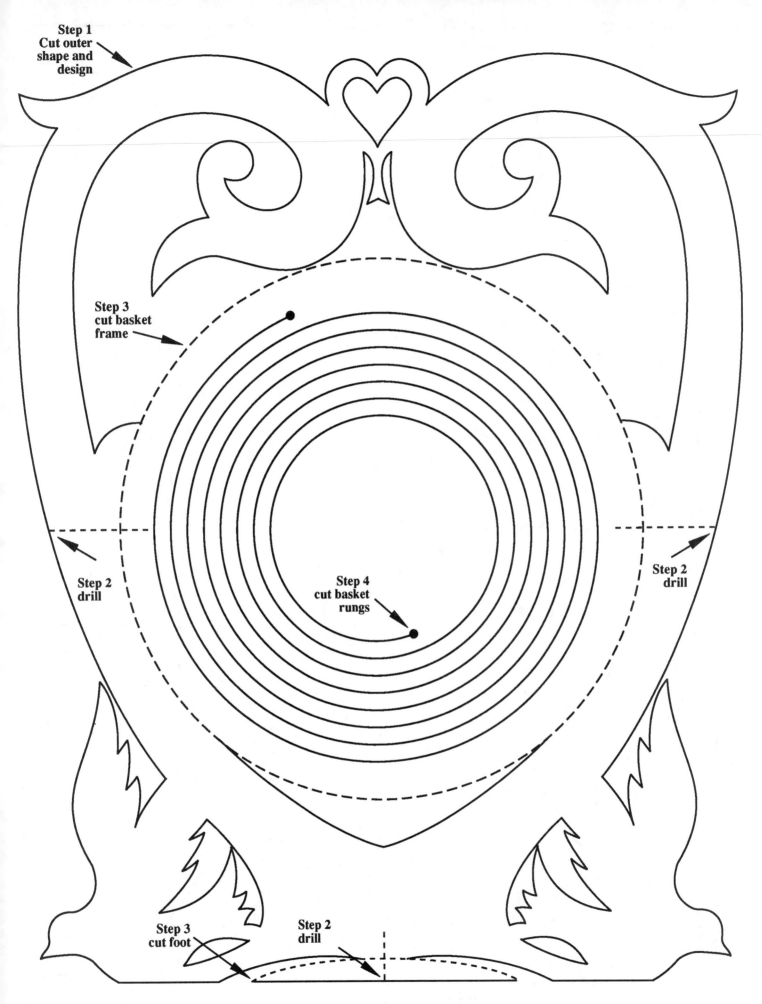

Step 1
Cut outer
shape and
design

Step 3
cut basket
frame

Step 2
drill

Step 2
drill

Step 4
cut basket
rungs

Step 3
cut foot

Step 2
drill

34

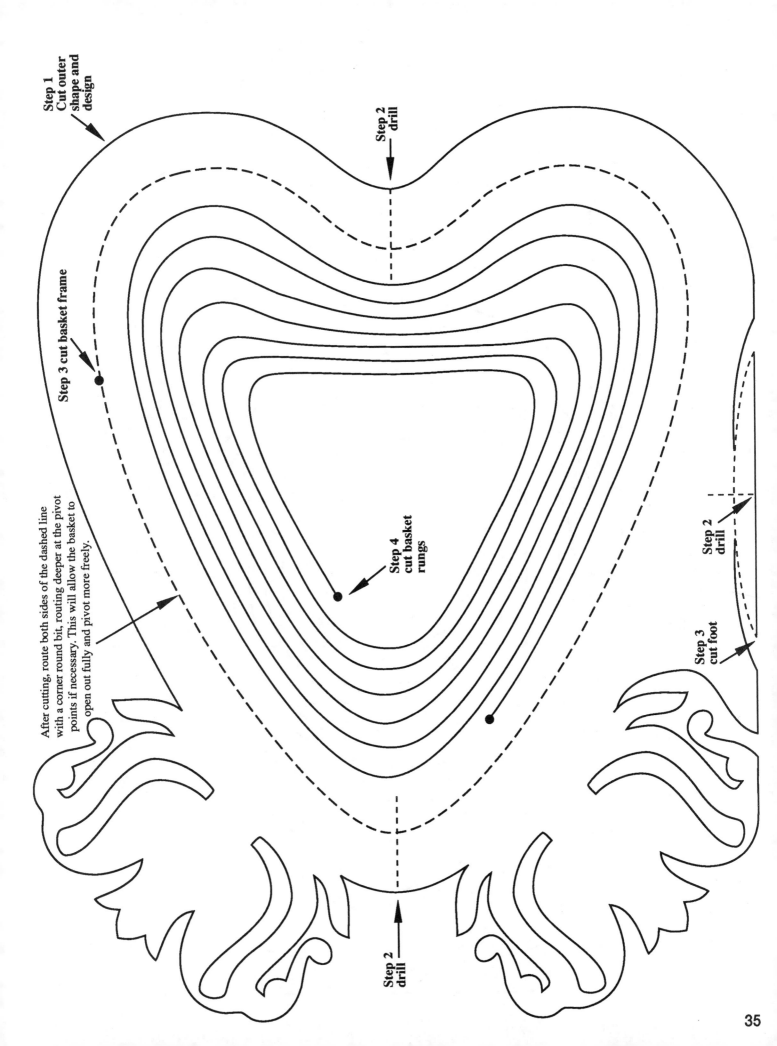

Step 1
Cut outer
shape and
design

Step 2
drill

Step 3 cut basket frame

After cutting, route both sides of the dashed line with a corner round bit, routing deeper at the pivot points if necessary. This will allow the basket to open out fully and pivot more freely.

Step 4
cut basket
rungs

Step 2
drill

Step 3
cut foot

Step 2
drill

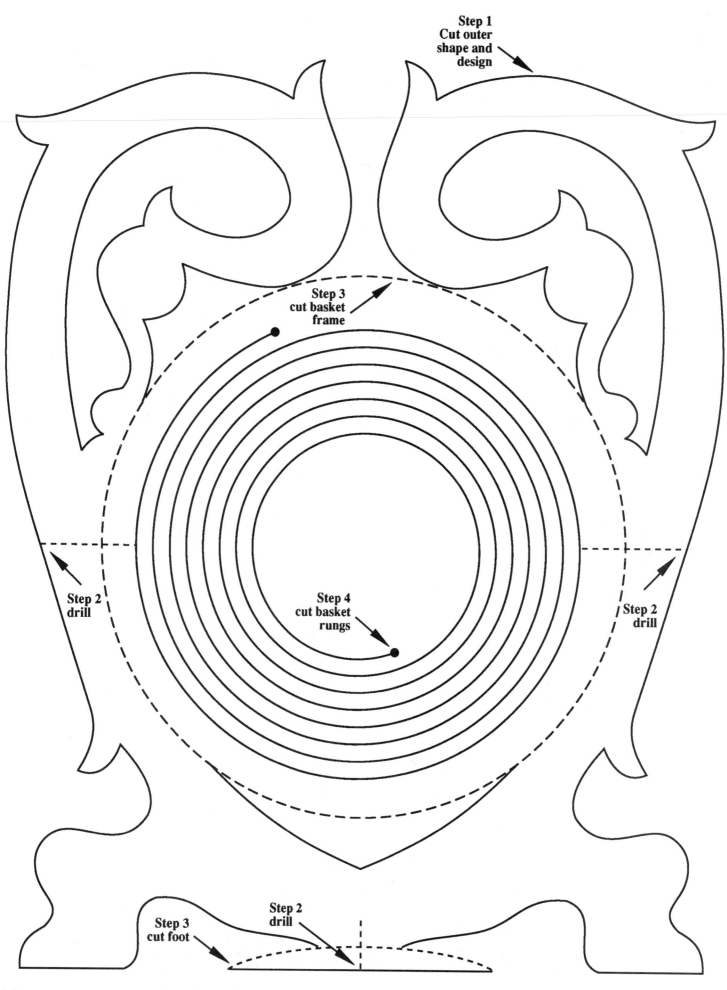

Step 1
Cut outer
shape and
design

Step 3
cut basket
frame

Step 2
drill

Step 4
cut basket
rungs

Step 2
drill

Step 3
cut foot

Step 2
drill

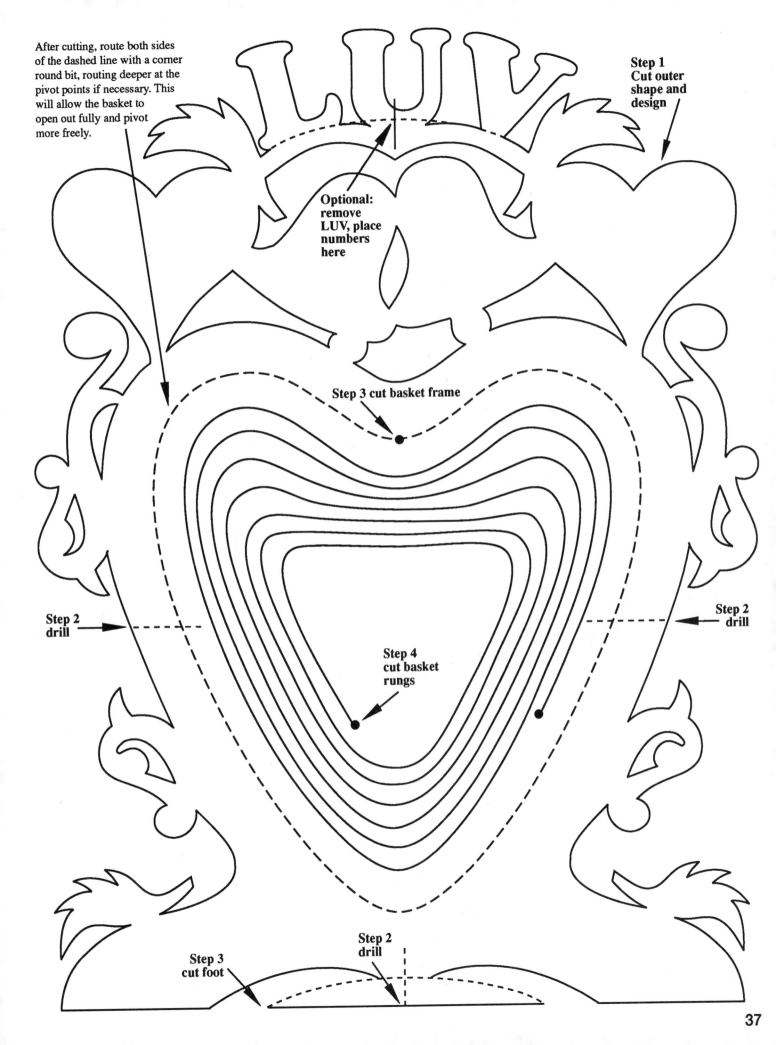

After cutting, route both sides of the dashed line with a corner round bit, routing deeper at the pivot points if necessary. This will allow the basket to open out fully and pivot more freely.

Step 1
Cut outer shape and design

Optional: remove LUV, place numbers here

Step 3 cut basket frame

Step 2 drill

Step 2 drill

Step 4 cut basket rungs

Step 3 cut foot

Step 2 drill

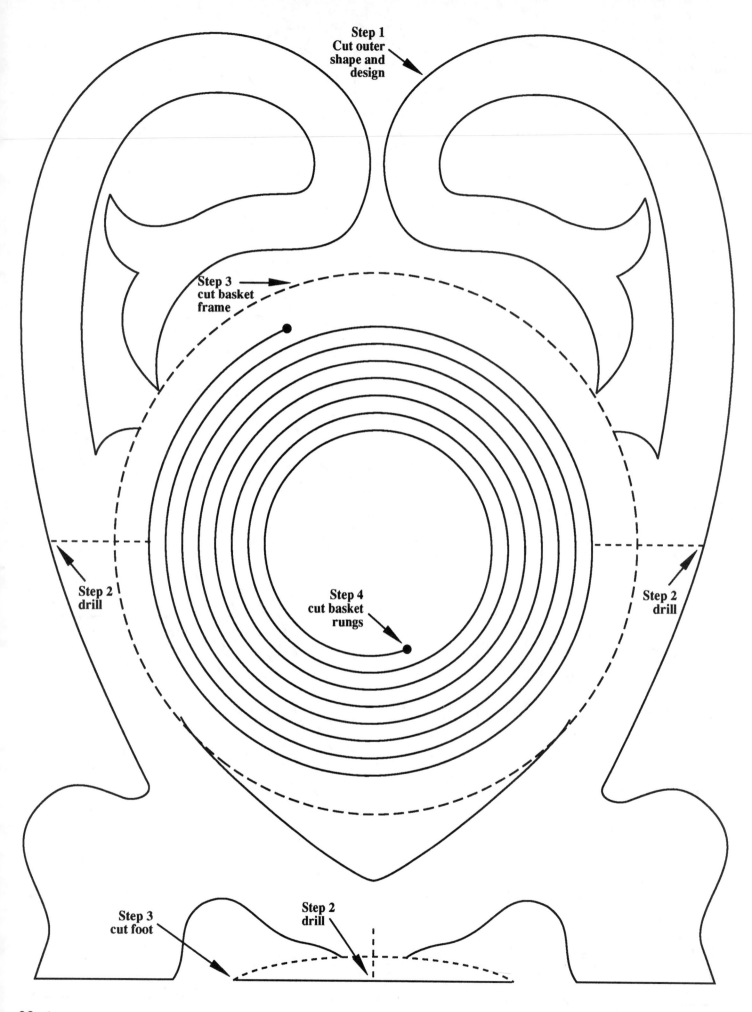

Step 1
Cut outer
shape and
design

Step 3
cut basket
frame

Step 2
drill

Step 4
cut basket
rungs

Step 2
drill

Step 3
cut foot

Step 2
drill

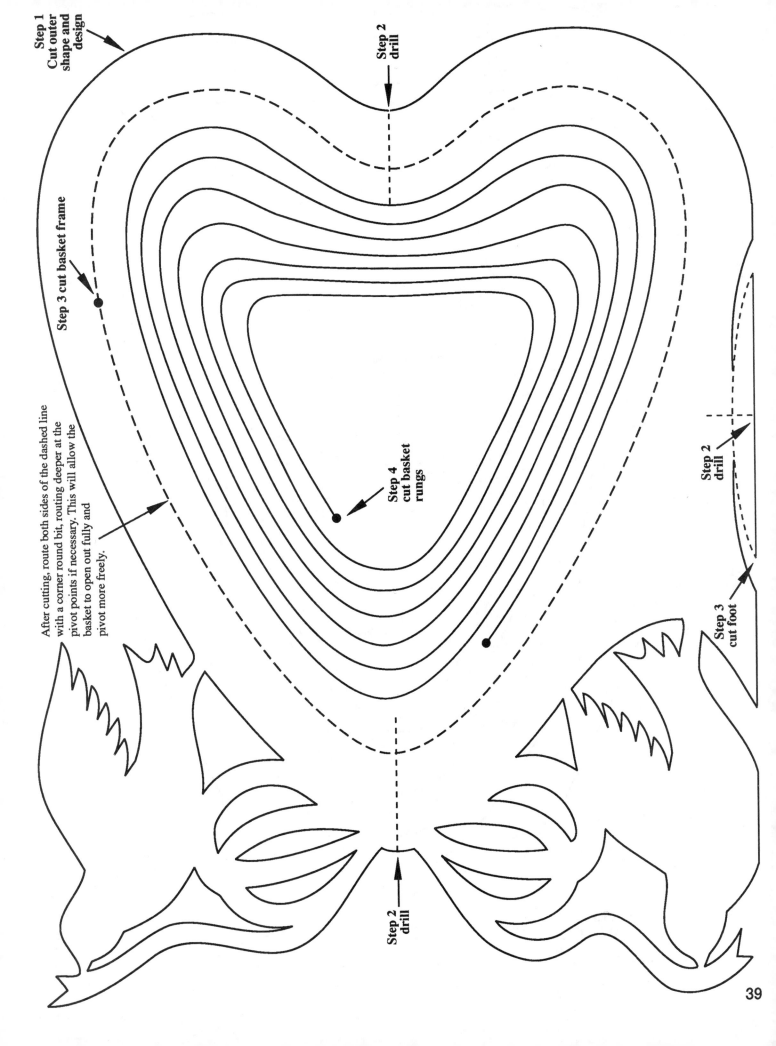

Step 1
Cut outer
shape and
design

Step 2
drill

Step 3 cut basket frame

After cutting, route both sides of the dashed line with a corner round bit, routing deeper at the pivot points if necessary. This will allow the basket to open out fully and pivot more freely.

Step 4
cut basket
rungs

Step 2
drill

Step 3
cut foot

Step 2
drill

39

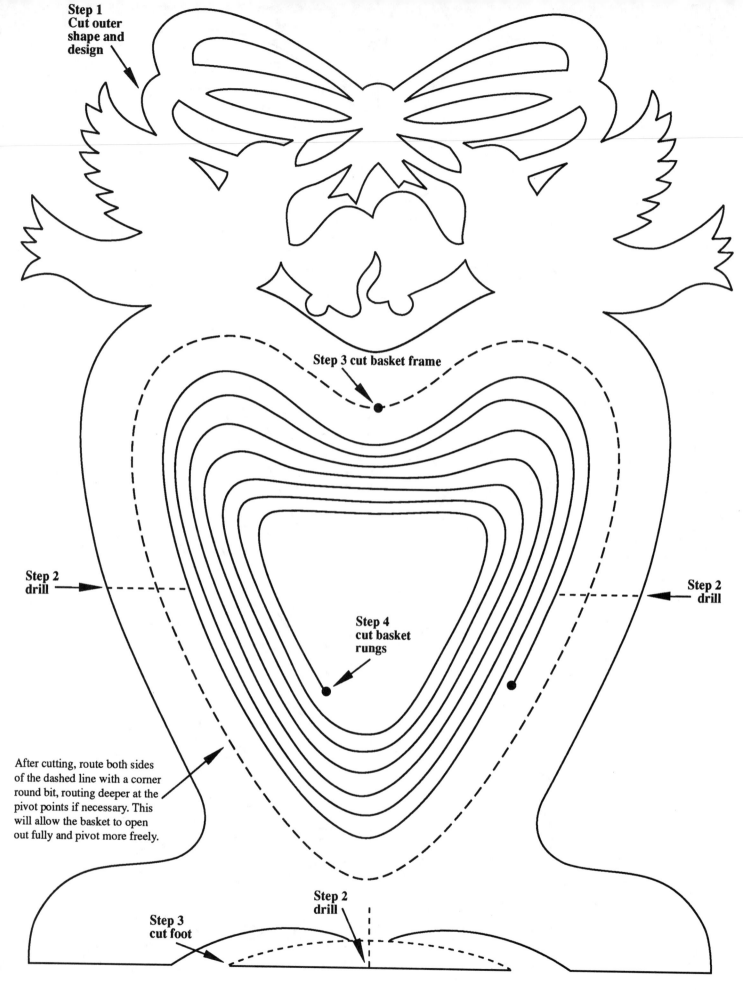

Step 1
Cut outer
shape and
design

Step 3 cut basket frame

Step 2
drill

Step 2
drill

Step 4
cut basket
rungs

After cutting, route both sides
of the dashed line with a corner
round bit, routing deeper at the
pivot points if necessary. This
will allow the basket to open
out fully and pivot more freely.

Step 2
drill

Step 3
cut foot

40

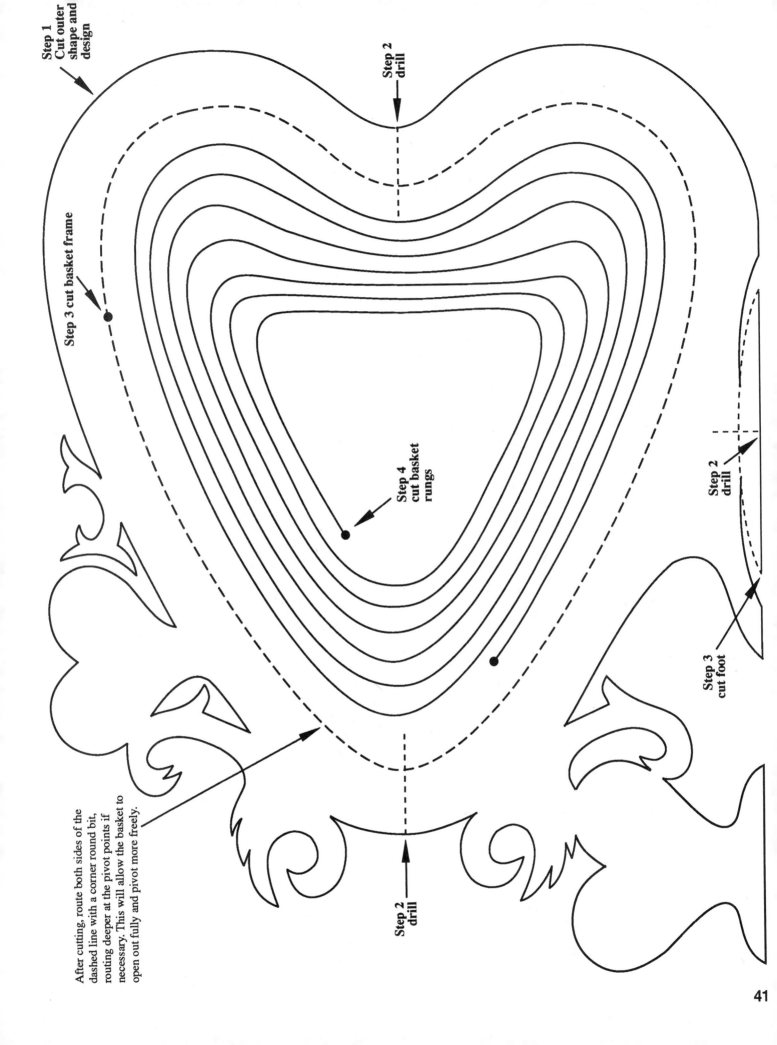

Step 1
Cut outer
shape and
design

Step 2
drill

Step 3 cut basket frame

Step 4
cut basket
rungs

Step 2
drill

Step 3
cut foot

After cutting, route both sides of the dashed line with a corner round bit, routing deeper at the pivot points if necessary. This will allow the basket to open out fully and pivot more freely.

Step 2
drill

41

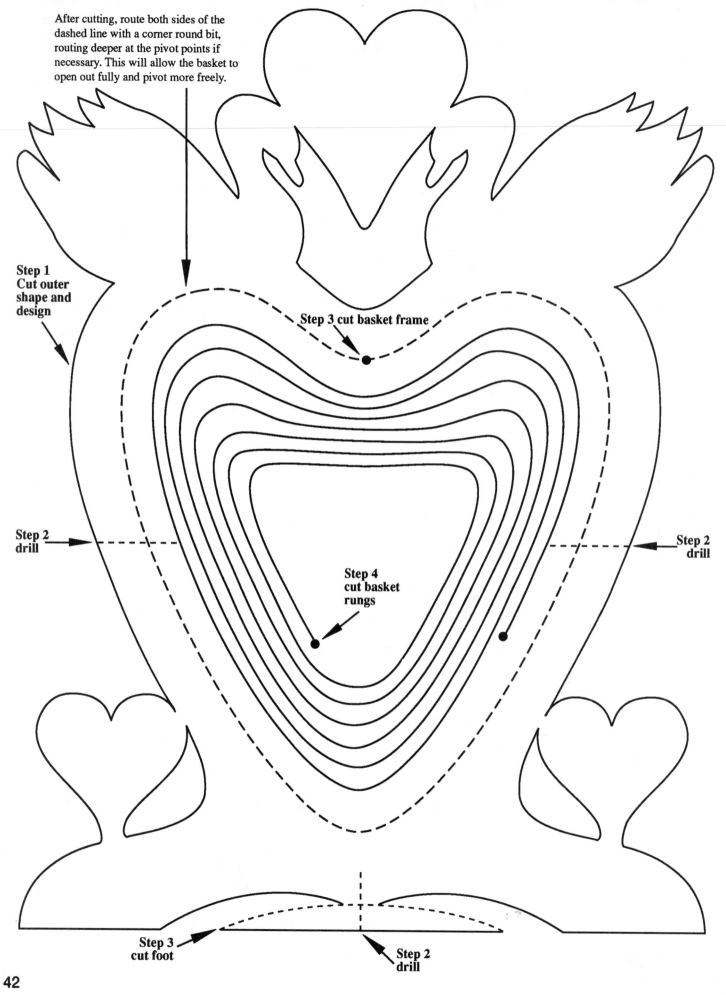

After cutting, route both sides of the dashed line with a corner round bit, routing deeper at the pivot points if necessary. This will allow the basket to open out fully and pivot more freely.

Step 1
Cut outer shape and design

Step 3 cut basket frame

Step 2 drill

Step 2 drill

Step 4 cut basket rungs

Step 3 cut foot

Step 2 drill

42

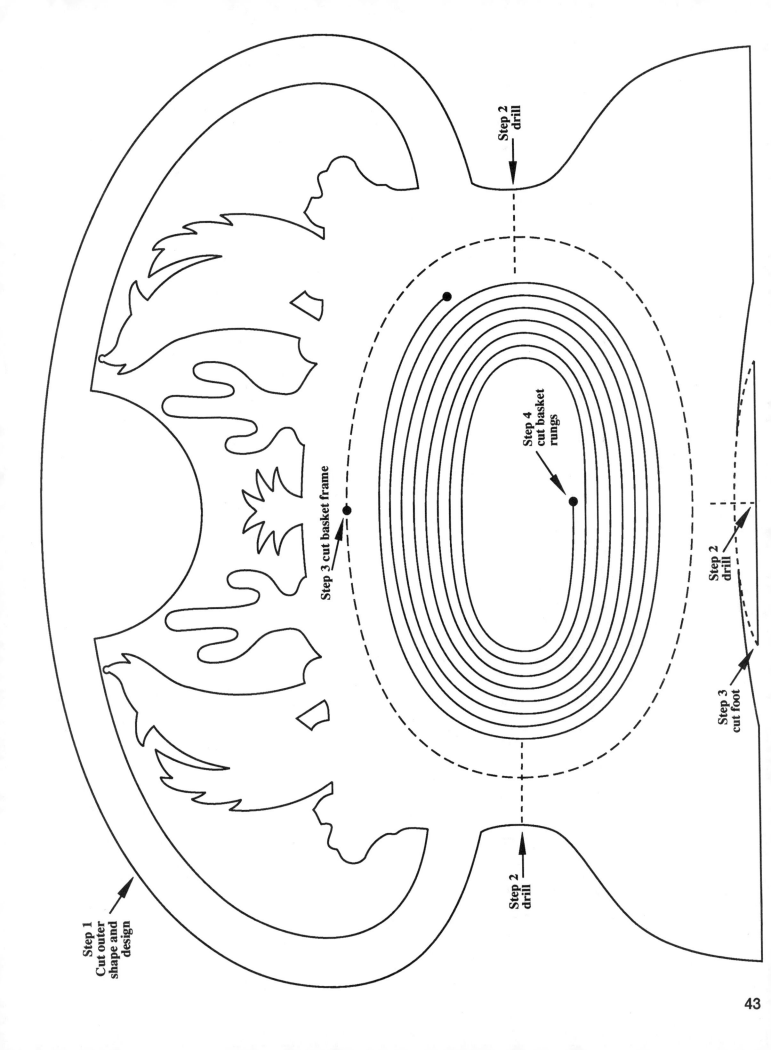

Step 2
drill

Step 3 cut basket frame

Step 4
cut basket
rungs

Step 2
drill

Step 3
cut foot

Step 2
drill

Step 1
Cut outer
shape and
design

43

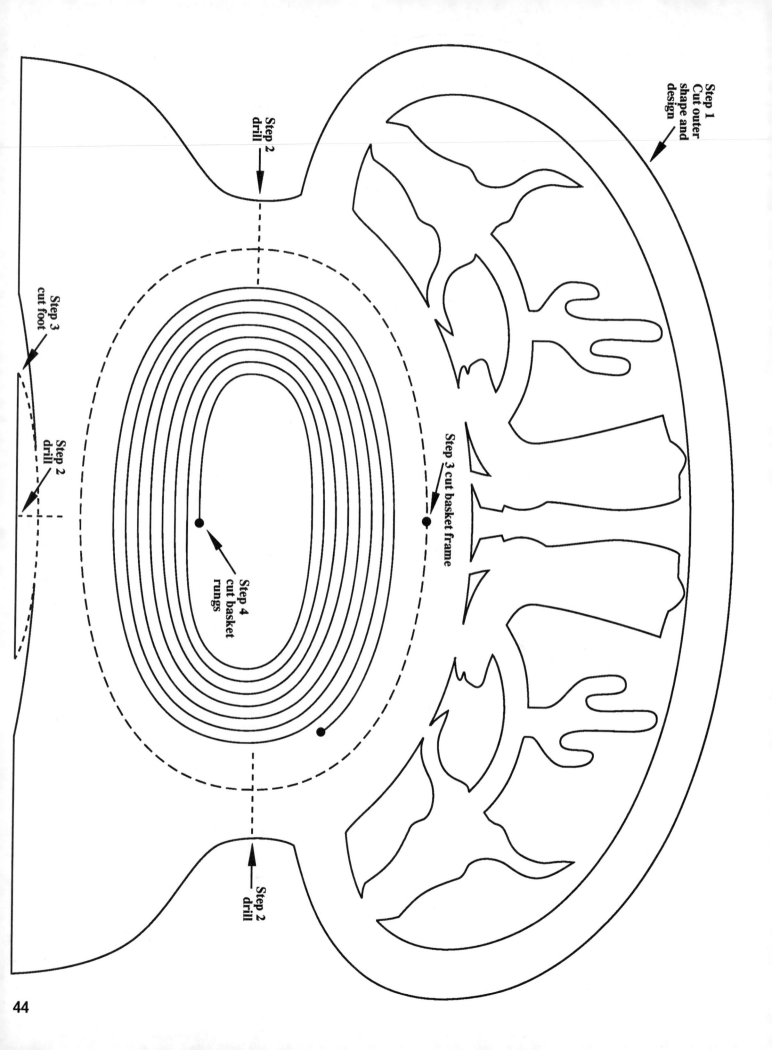

Step 1
Cut outer
shape and
design

Step 2
drill

Step 3
cut foot

Step 2
drill

Step 3 cut basket frame

Step 4
cut basket
rungs

Step 2
drill

44

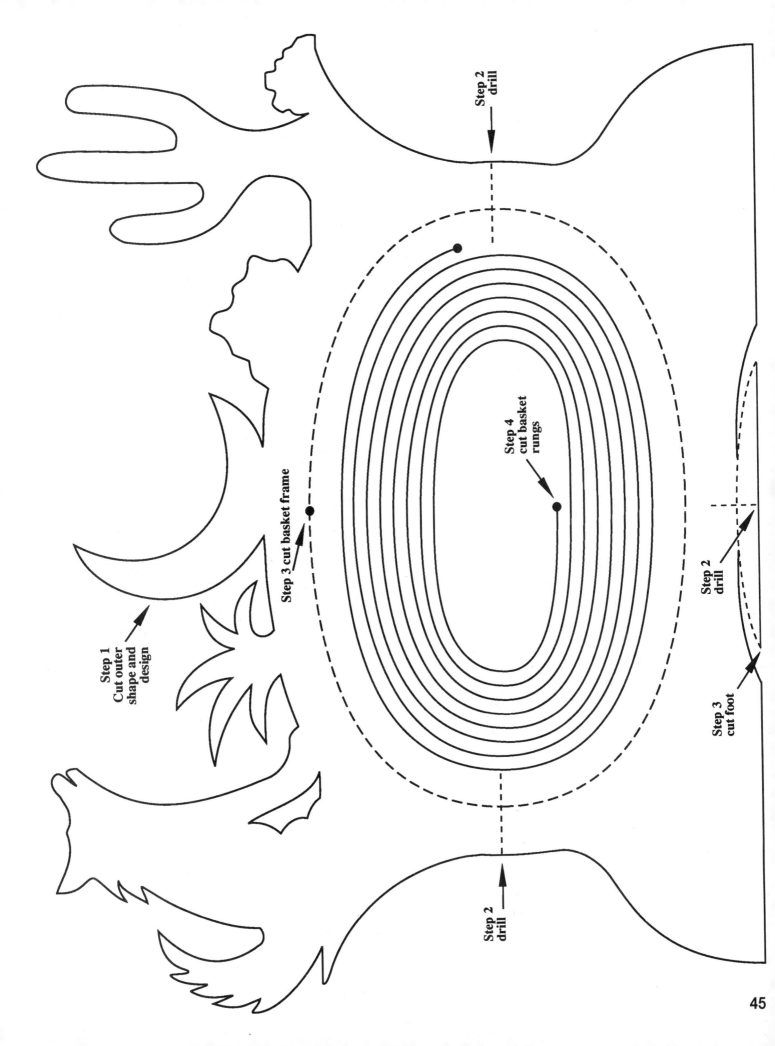

Step 2 drill

Step 1 Cut outer shape and design

Step 3 cut basket frame

Step 4 cut basket rungs

Step 2 drill

Step 3 cut foot

Step 2 drill

45

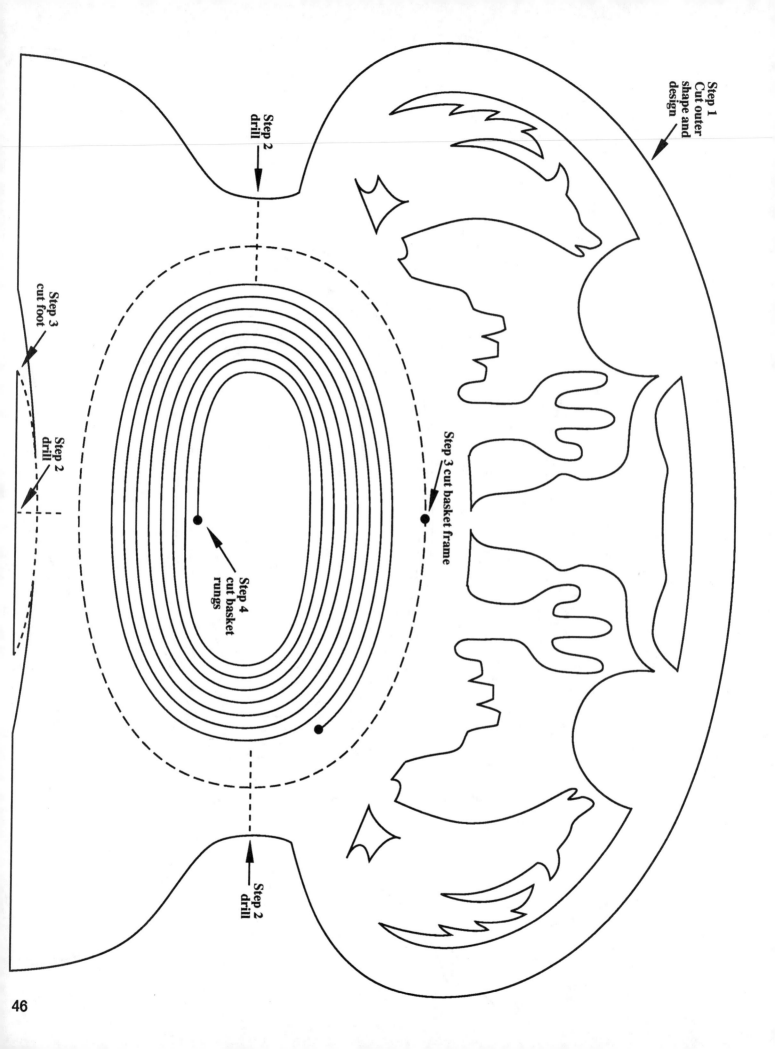

Step 1
Cut outer
shape and
design

Step 2
drill

Step 3
cut foot

Step 2
drill

Step 3 cut basket frame

Step 4
cut basket
rungs

Step 2
drill

46

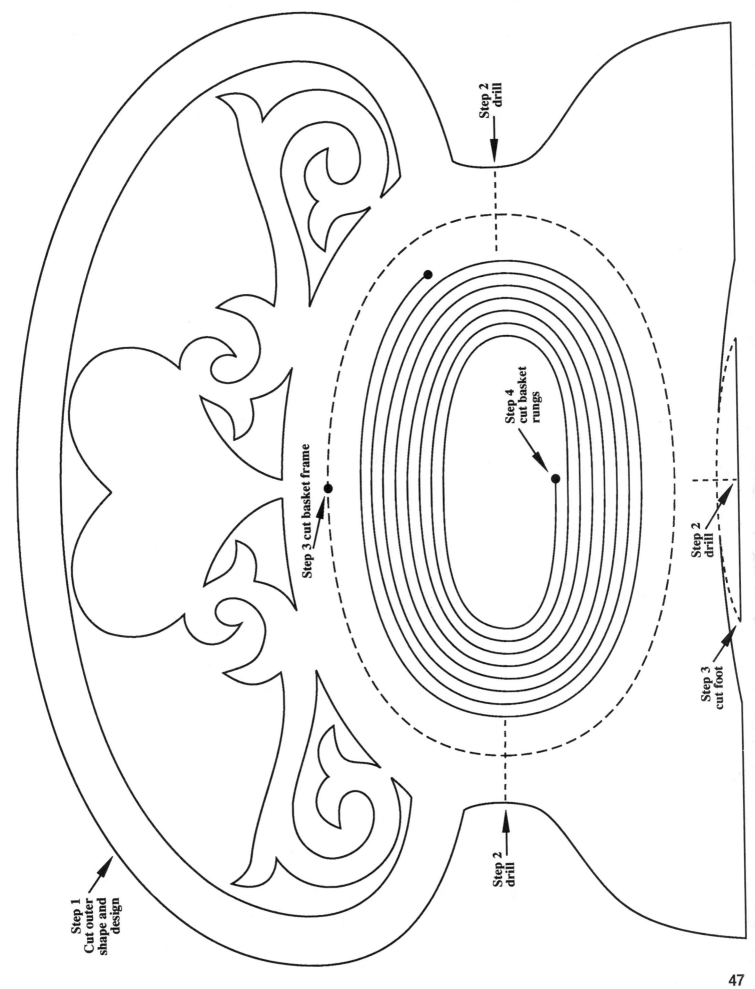

Step 2
drill

Step 3 cut basket frame

Step 4
cut basket
rungs

Step 2
drill

Step 3
cut foot

Step 2
drill

Step 1
Cut outer
shape and
design

47

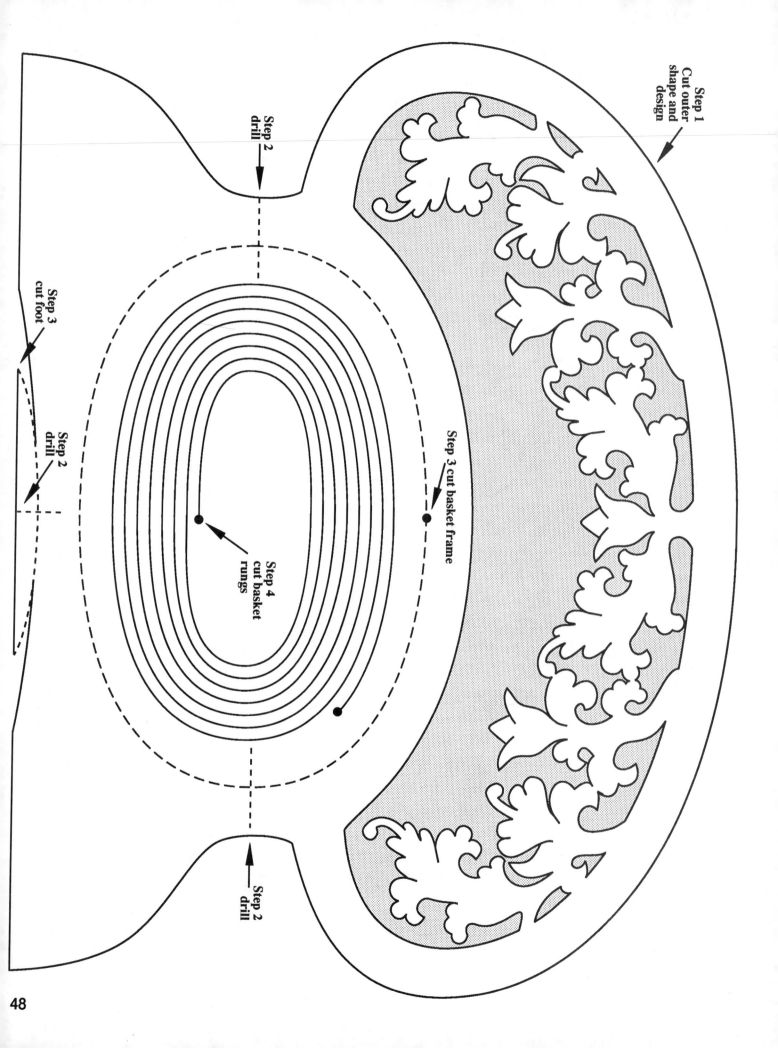

Step 1
Cut outer
shape and
design

Step 2
drill

Step 3
cut foot

Step 2
drill

Step 3 cut basket frame

Step 4
cut basket
rungs

Step 2
drill

48

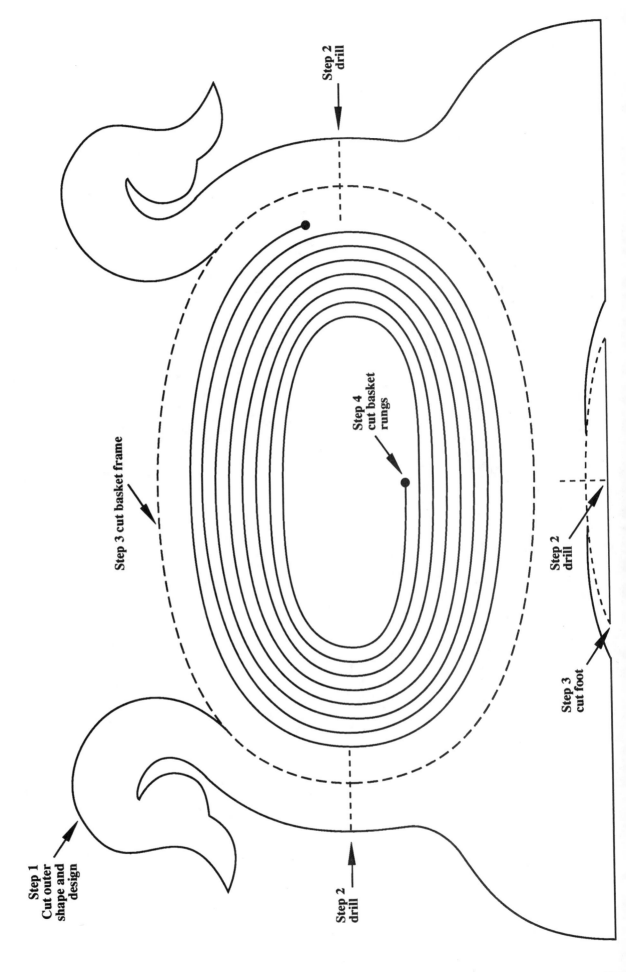

Step 2
drill

Step 1
Cut outer
shape and
design

Step 3 cut basket frame

Step 4
cut basket
rungs

Step 2
drill

Step 3
cut foot

Step 2
drill

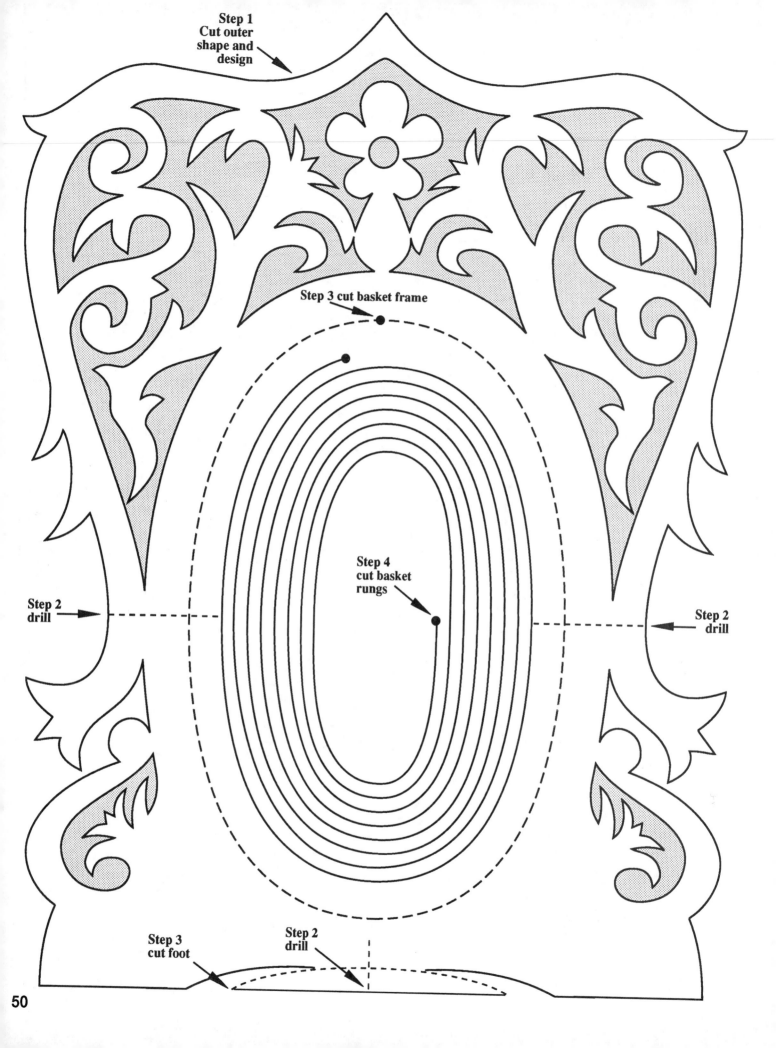

Step 1
Cut outer
shape and
design

Step 3 cut basket frame

Step 4
cut basket
rungs

Step 2
drill

Step 2
drill

Step 3
cut foot

Step 2
drill

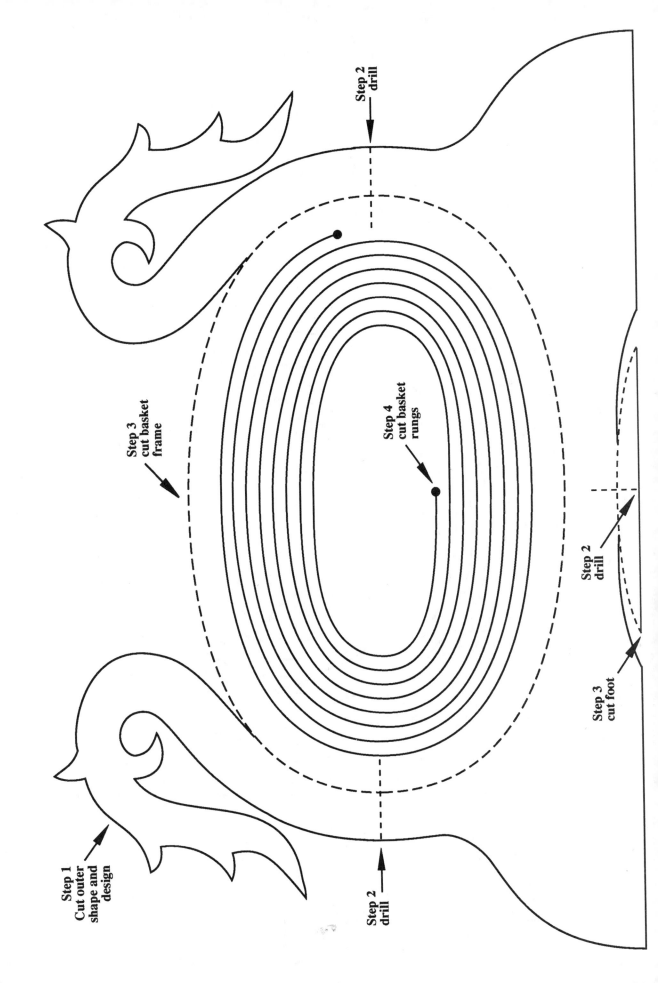

Step 2
drill

Step 3
cut basket
frame

Step 4
cut basket
rungs

Step 2
drill

Step 3
cut foot

Step 1
Cut outer
shape and
design

Step 2
drill

51

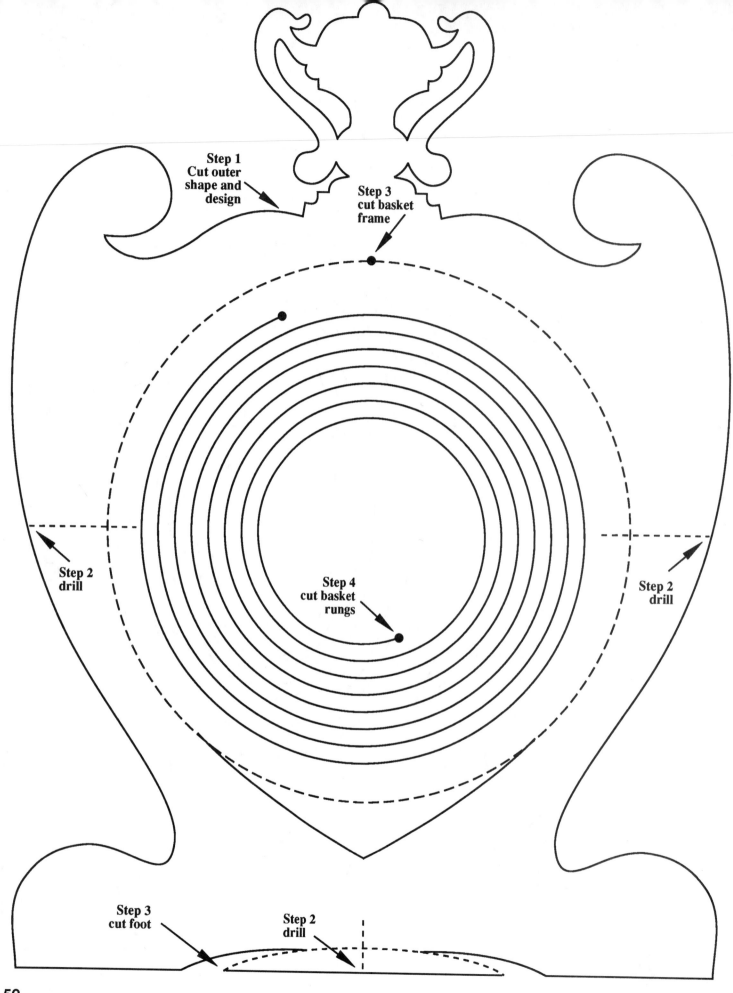

Step 1
Cut outer
shape and
design

Step 3
cut basket
frame

Step 2
drill

Step 2
drill

Step 4
cut basket
rungs

Step 3
cut foot

Step 2
drill

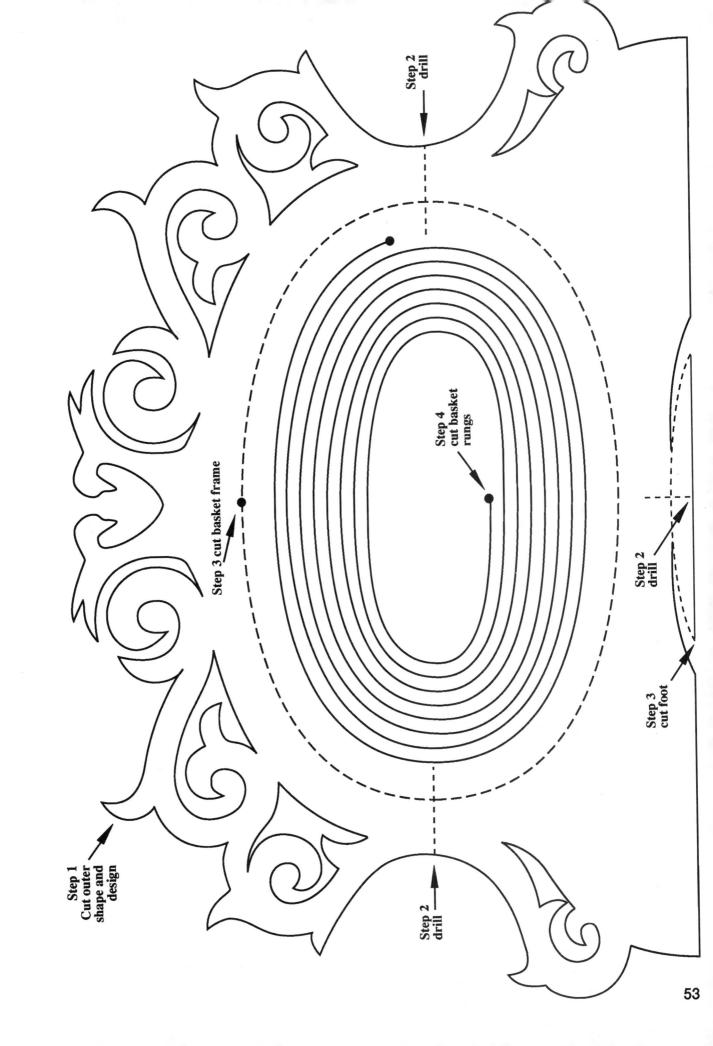

Step 2
drill

Step 4
cut basket
rungs

Step 3 cut basket frame

Step 2
drill

Step 3
cut foot

Step 1
Cut outer
shape and
design

Step 2
drill

53

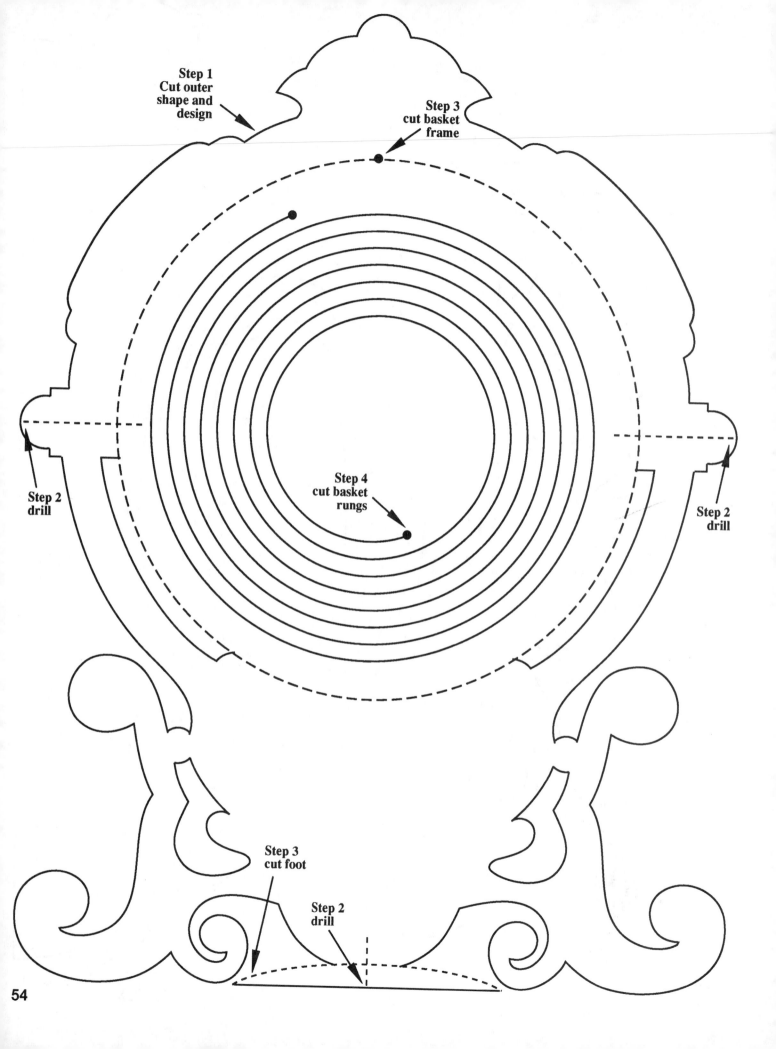

Step 1
Cut outer
shape and
design

Step 3
cut basket
frame

Step 2
drill

Step 4
cut basket
rungs

Step 2
drill

Step 3
cut foot

Step 2
drill

54

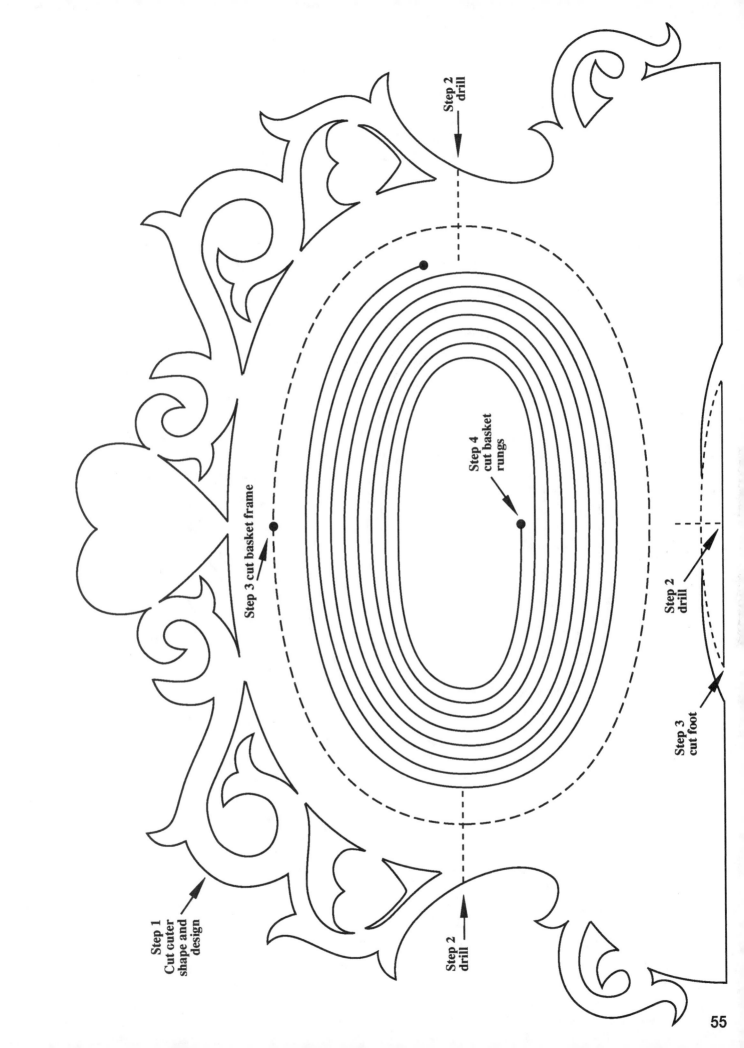

Step 2
drill

Step 4
cut basket
rungs

Step 3 cut basket frame

Step 2
drill

Step 2
drill

Step 3
cut foot

Step 1
Cut outer
shape and
design

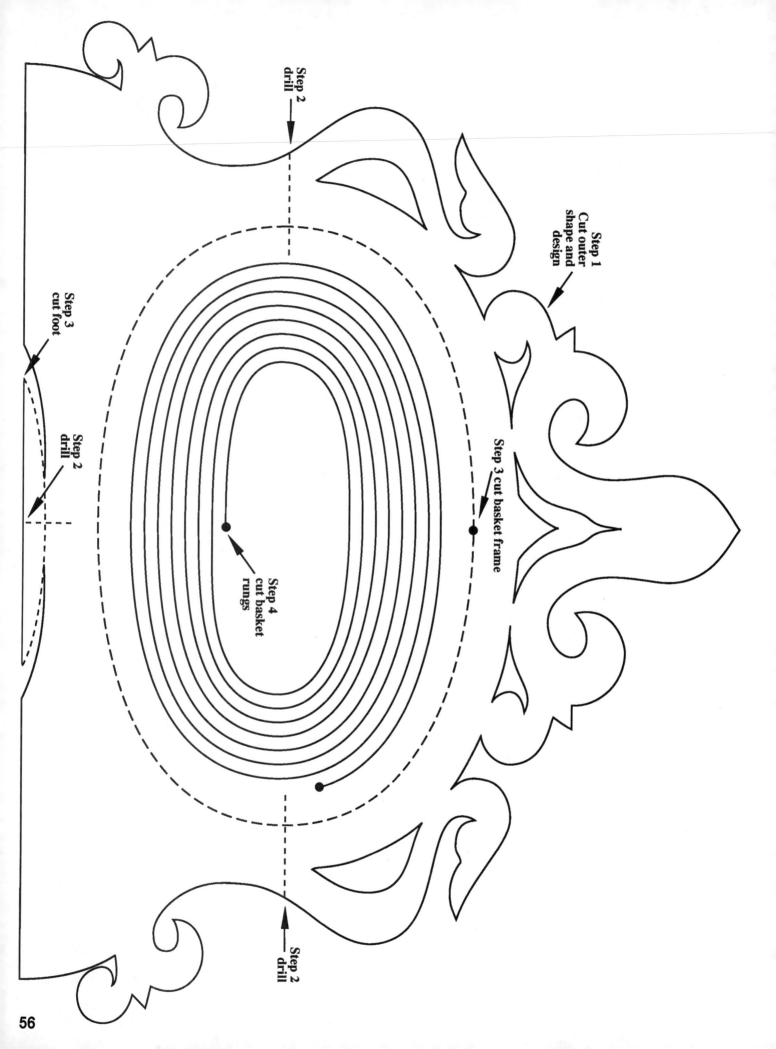

Step 2
drill

Step 1
Cut outer
shape and
design

Step 3
cut foot

Step 2
drill

Step 3 cut basket frame

Step 4
cut basket
rungs

Step 2
drill

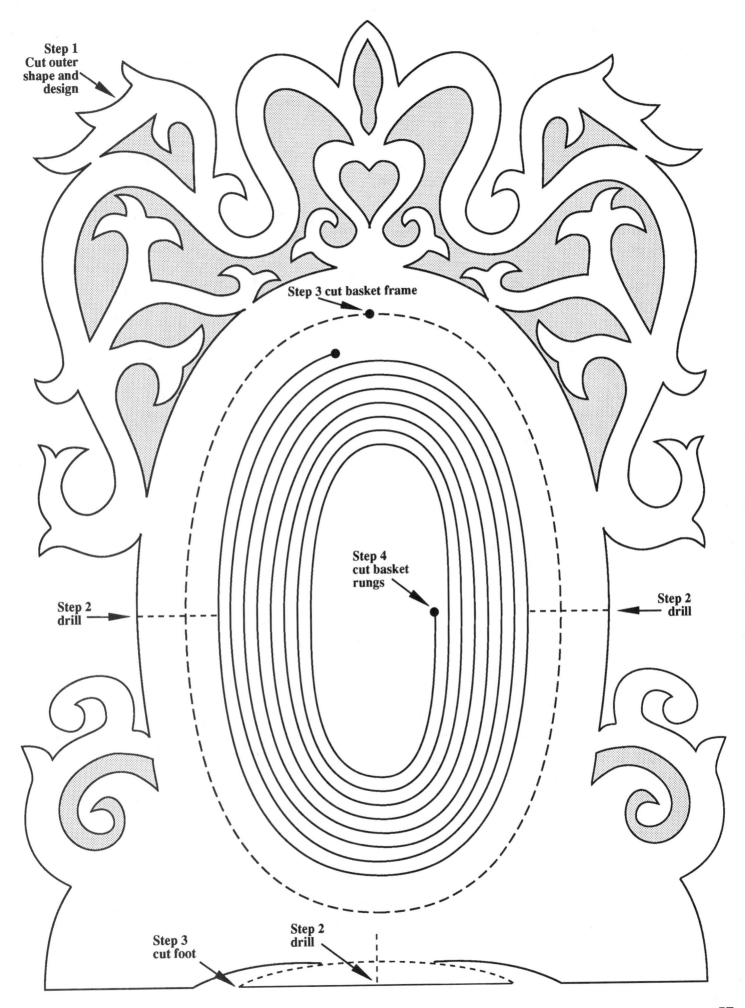

Step 1
Cut outer
shape and
design

Step 3 cut basket frame

Step 4
cut basket
rungs

Step 2
drill

Step 2
drill

Step 3
cut foot

Step 2
drill

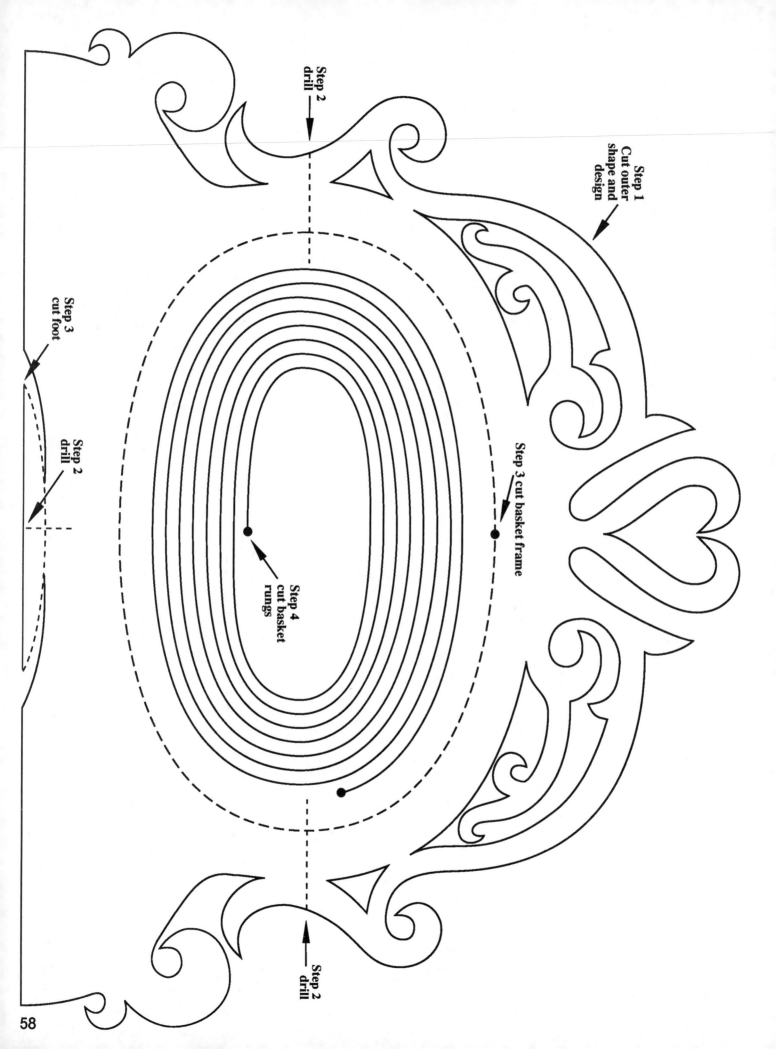

Step 2
drill

Step 1
Cut outer
shape and
design

Step 3
cut foot

Step 2
drill

Step 3 cut basket frame

Step 4
cut basket
rungs

Step 2
drill

58

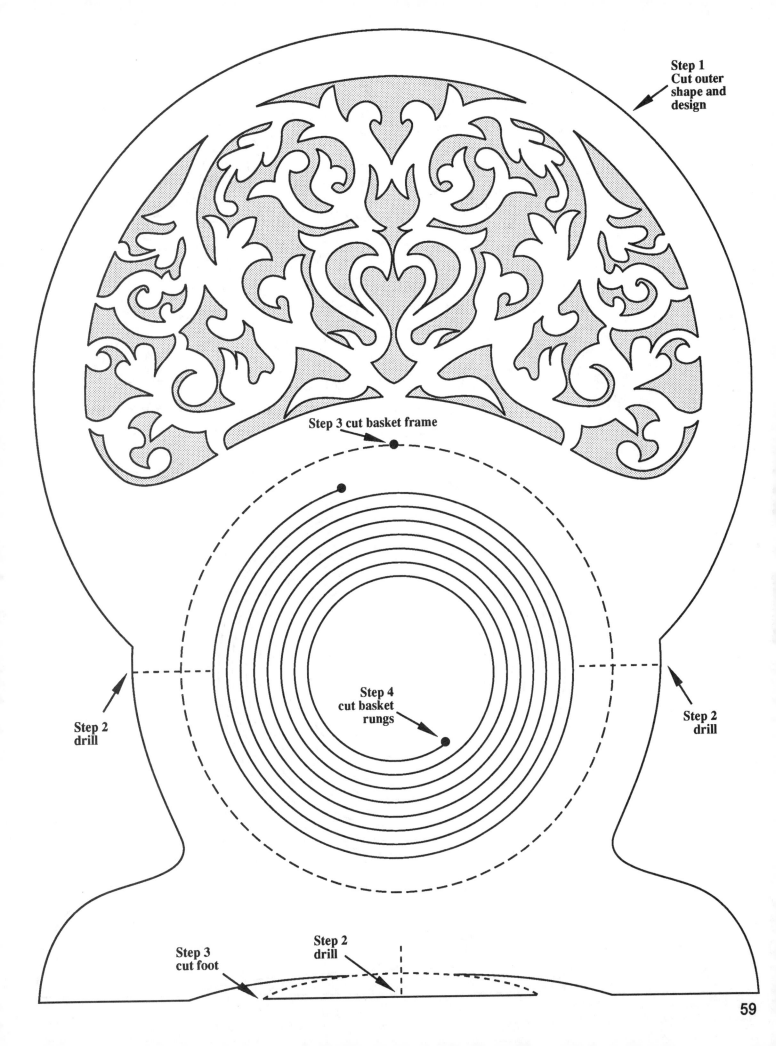

Step 1
Cut outer
shape and
design

Step 3 cut basket frame

Step 2
drill

Step 4
cut basket
rungs

Step 2
drill

Step 3
cut foot

Step 2
drill

59

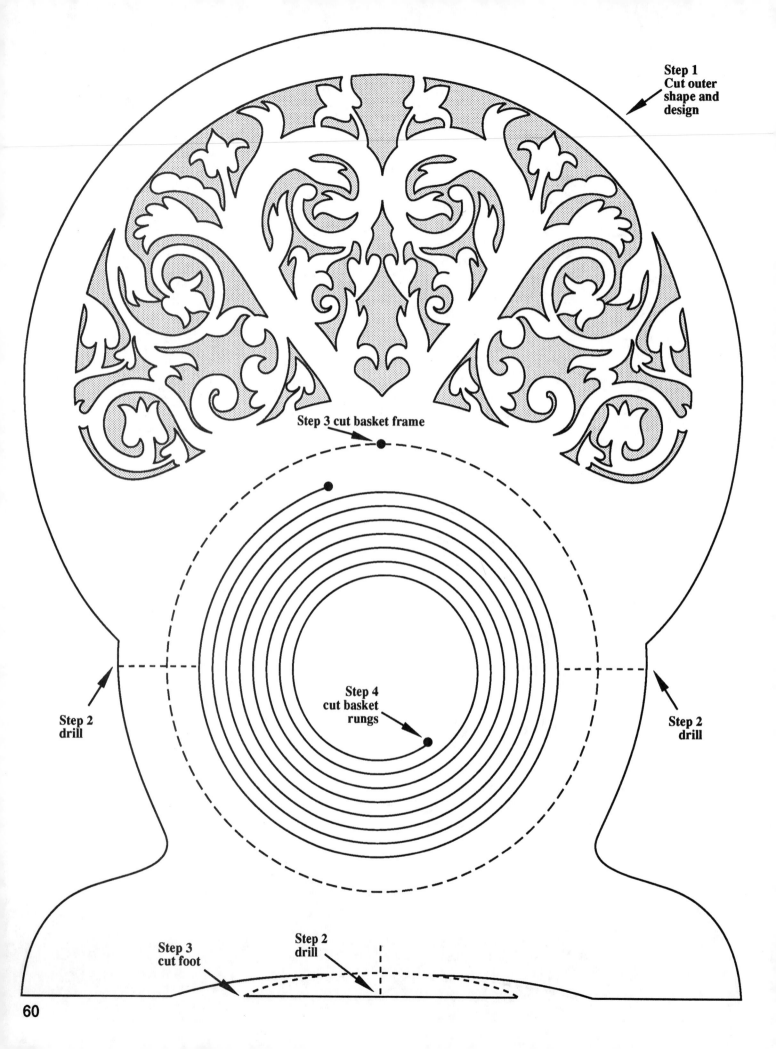

Step 1
Cut outer
shape and
design

Step 3 cut basket frame

Step 2
drill

Step 4
cut basket
rungs

Step 2
drill

Step 3
cut foot

Step 2
drill

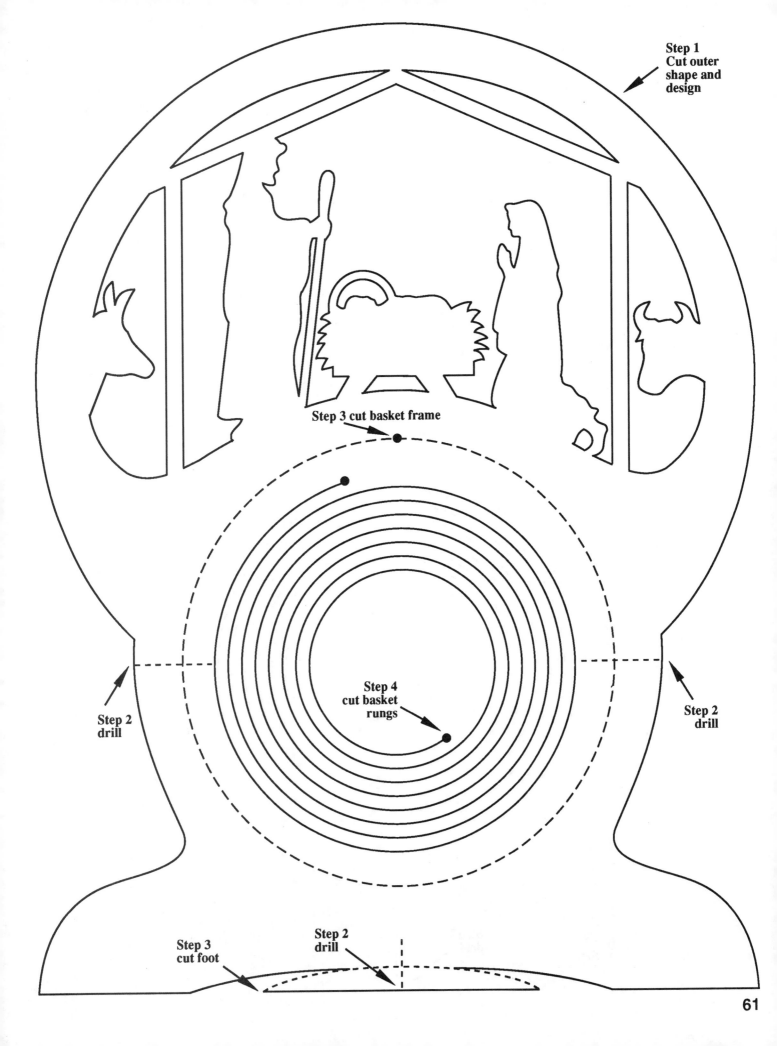

Step 1
Cut outer
shape and
design

Step 3 cut basket frame

Step 4
cut basket
rungs

Step 2
drill

Step 2
drill

Step 3
cut foot

Step 2
drill

61

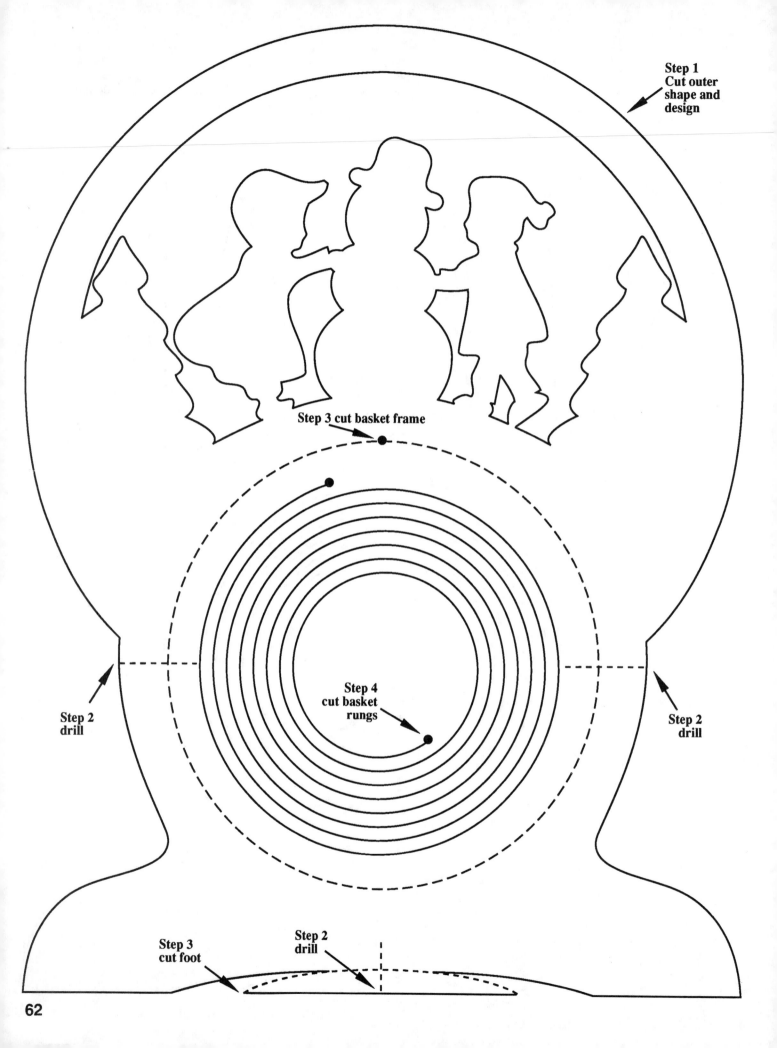

Step 1
Cut outer
shape and
design

Step 3 cut basket frame

Step 2
drill

Step 4
cut basket
rungs

Step 2
drill

Step 3
cut foot

Step 2
drill

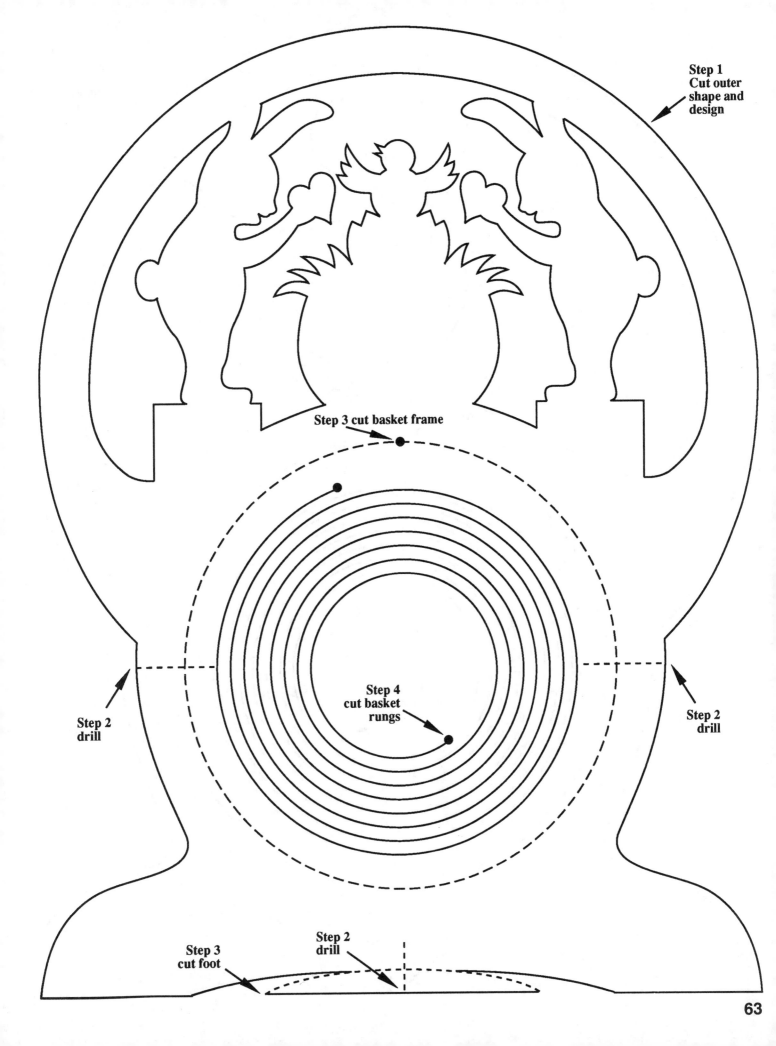

Step 1
Cut outer
shape and
design

Step 3 cut basket frame

Step 2
drill

Step 4
cut basket
rungs

Step 2
drill

Step 3
cut foot

Step 2
drill

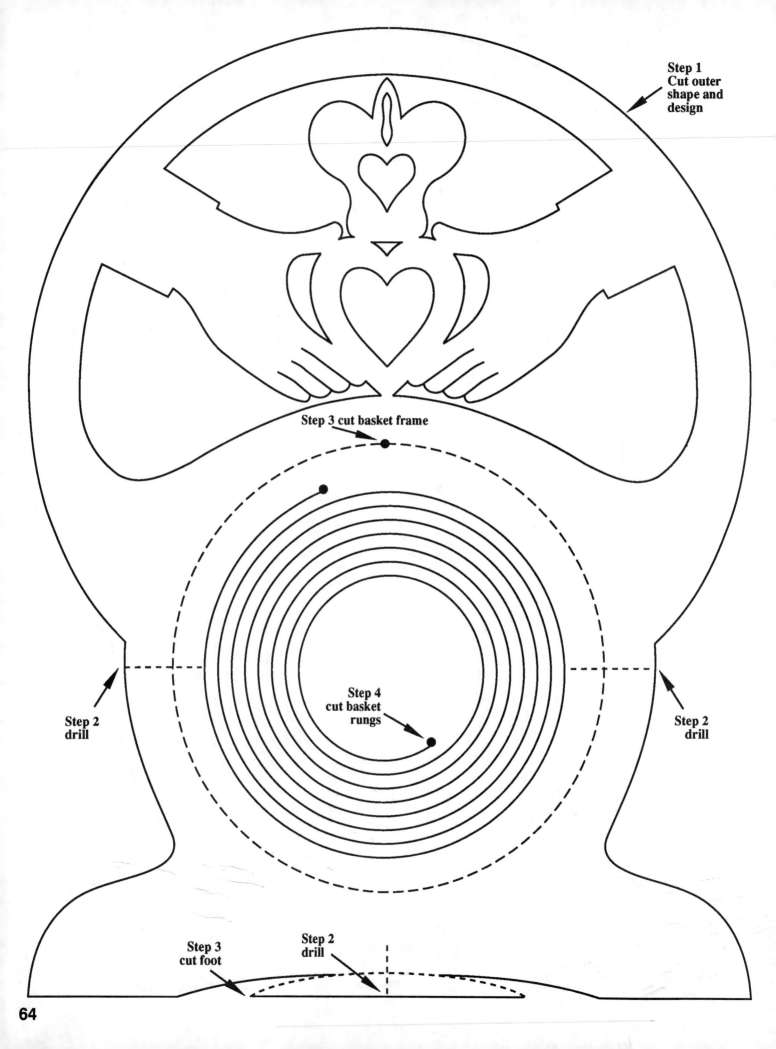

Step 1
Cut outer
shape and
design

Step 3 cut basket frame

Step 2
drill

Step 2
drill

Step 4
cut basket
rungs

Step 3
cut foot

Step 2
drill

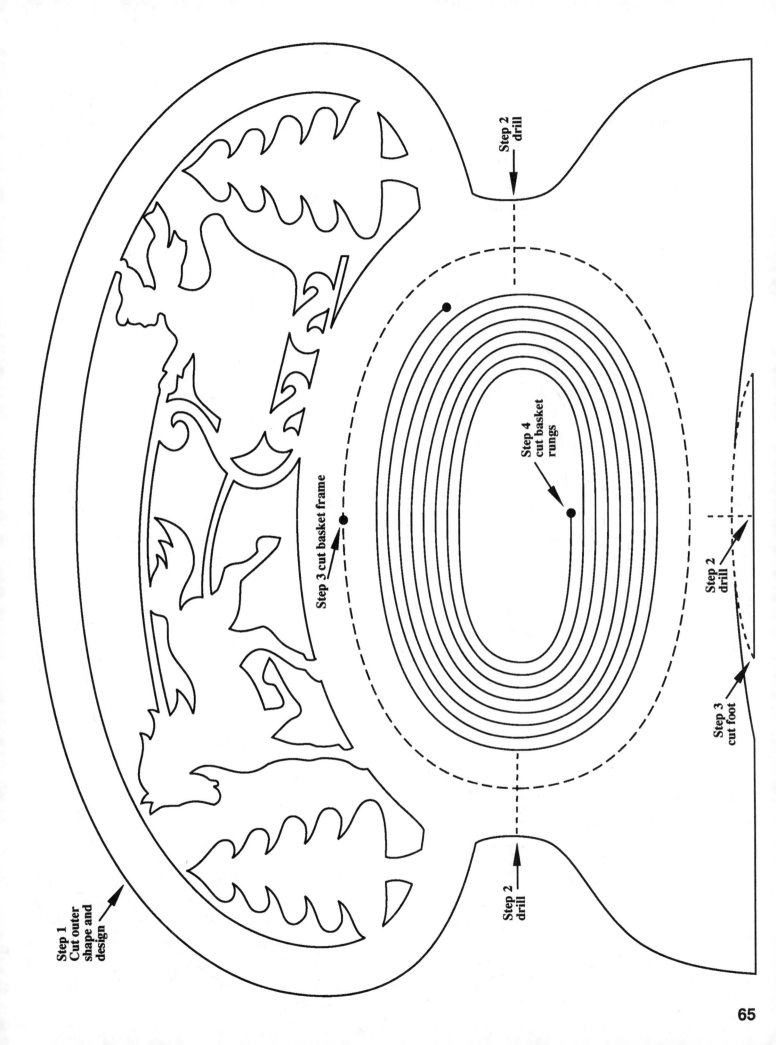

Step 2
drill

Step 1
Cut outer
shape and
design

Step 3 cut basket frame

Step 4
cut basket
rungs

Step 2
drill

Step 2
drill

Step 3
cut foot

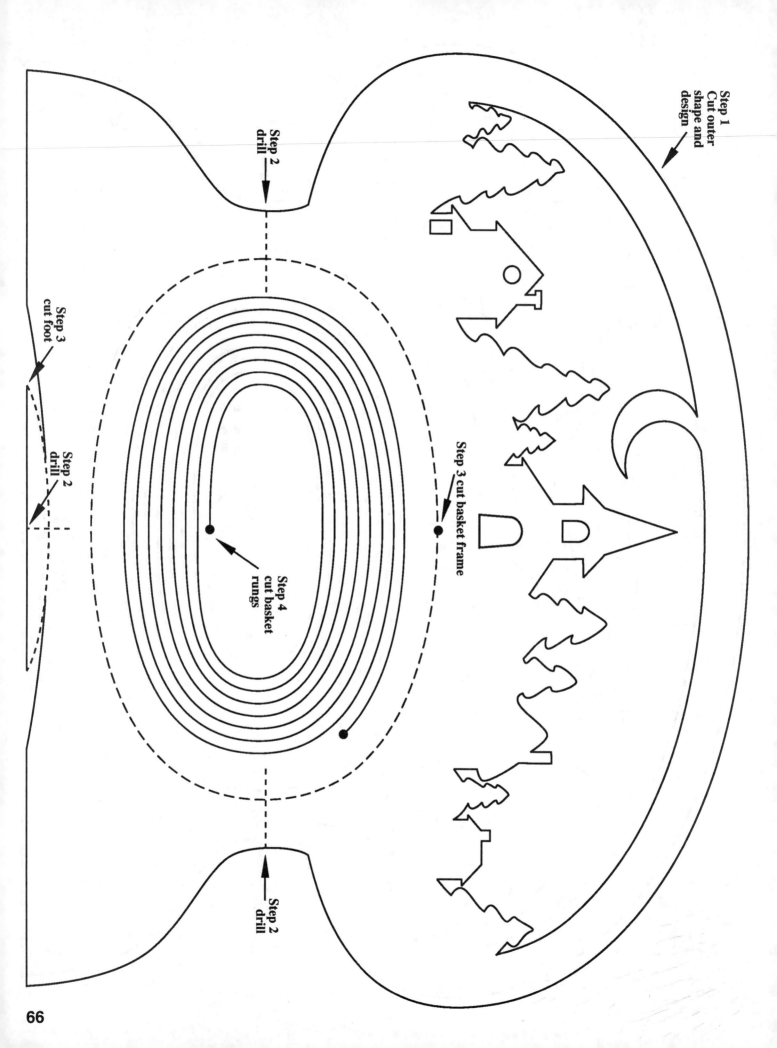

Step 1
Cut outer
shape and
design

Step 2
drill

Step 3
cut foot

Step 2
drill

Step 3 cut basket frame

Step 4
cut basket
rungs

Step 2
drill

Step 2
drill

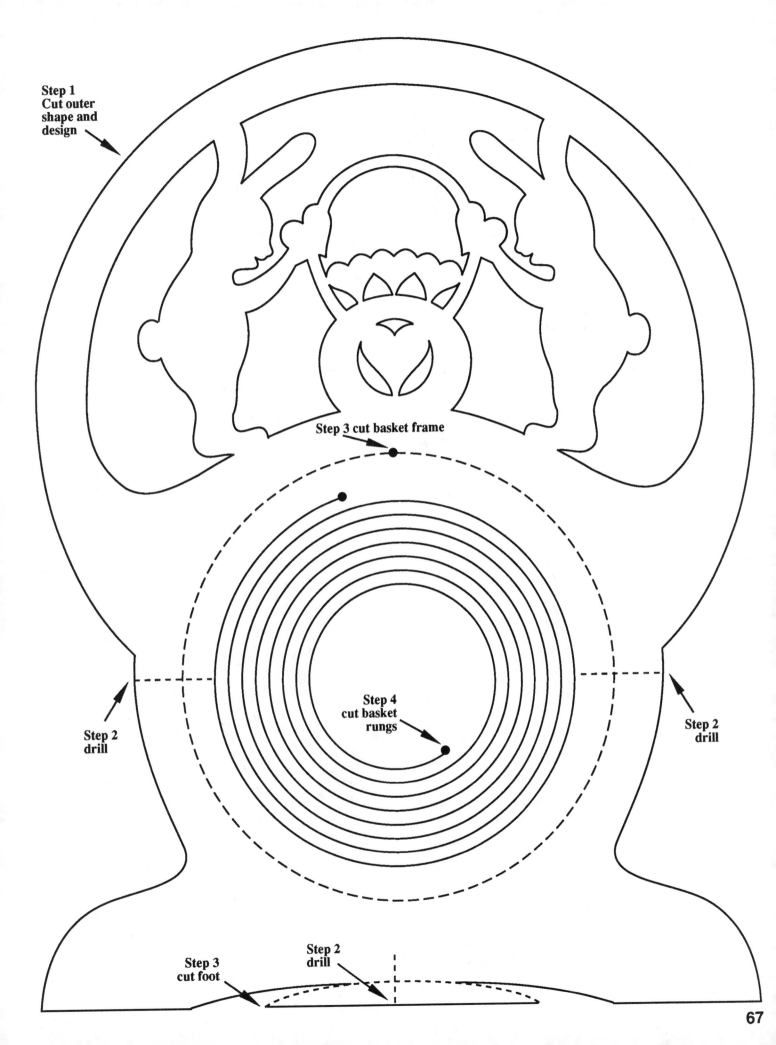

Step 1
Cut outer
shape and
design

Step 3 cut basket frame

Step 2
drill

Step 4
cut basket
rungs

Step 2
drill

Step 3
cut foot

Step 2
drill

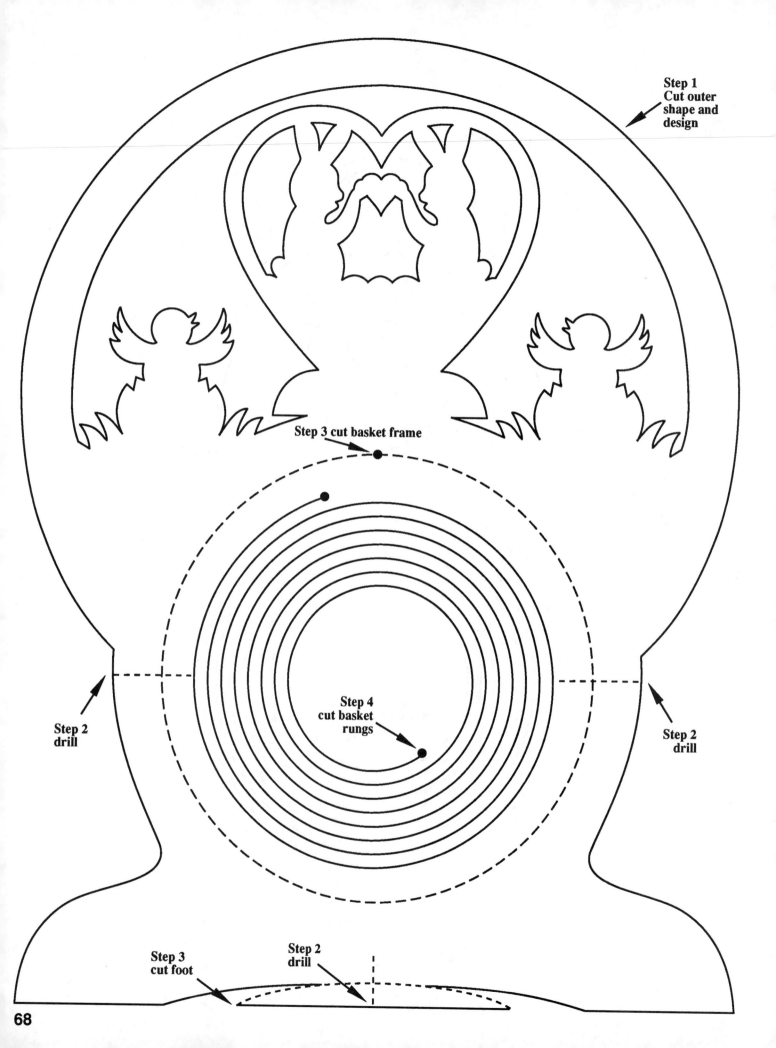

Step 1
Cut outer
shape and
design

Step 3 cut basket frame

Step 2
drill

Step 4
cut basket
rungs

Step 2
drill

Step 3
cut foot

Step 2
drill

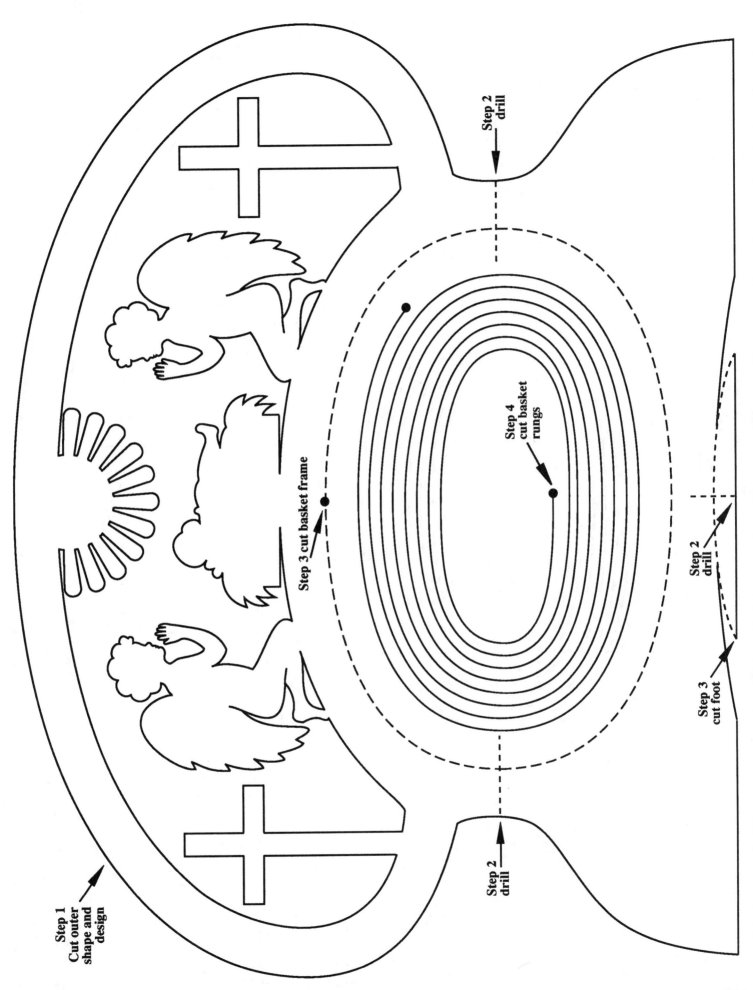

Step 1
Cut outer
shape and
design

Step 3 cut basket frame

Step 4
cut basket
rungs

Step 2
drill

Step 2
drill

Step 2
drill

Step 3
cut foot

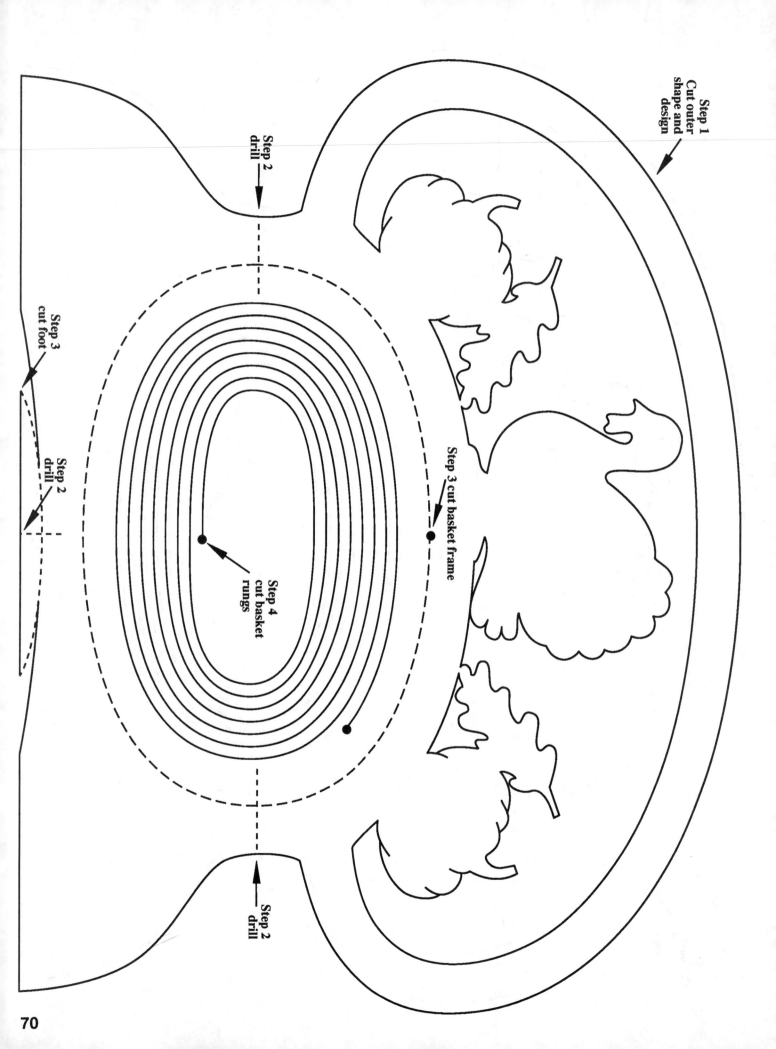

Step 1
Cut outer
shape and
design

Step 2
drill

Step 3
cut foot

Step 2
drill

Step 3 cut basket frame

Step 4
cut basket
rungs

Step 2
drill

70

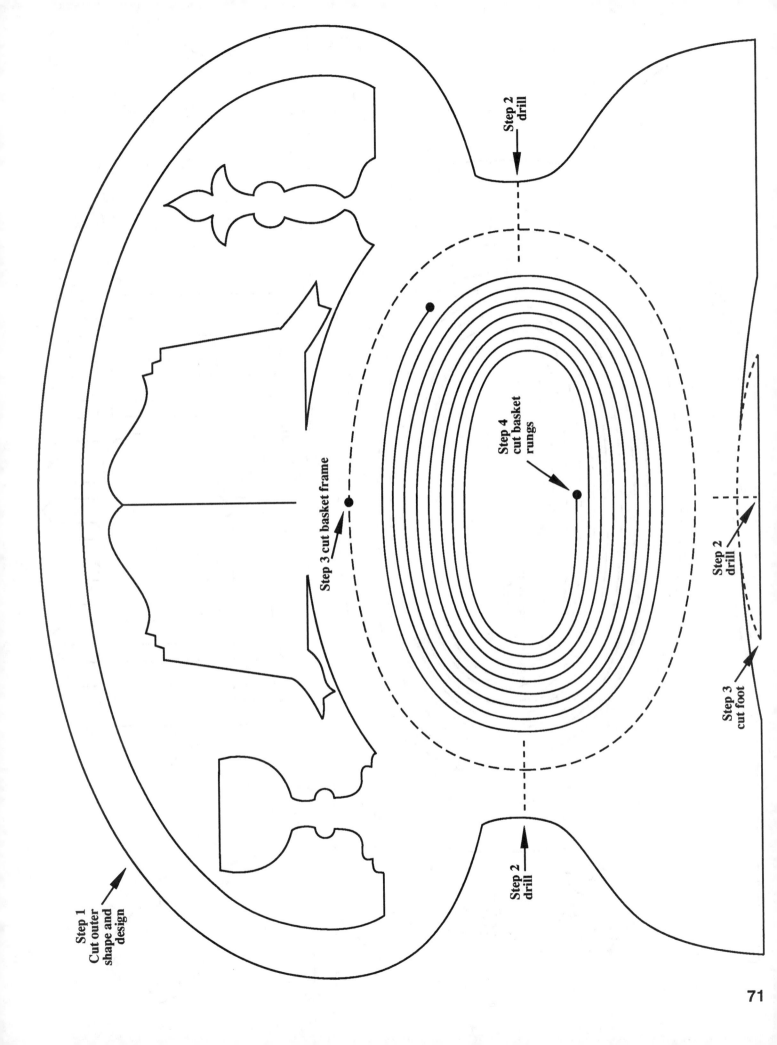

Step 2
drill

Step 1
Cut outer
shape and
design

Step 3 cut basket frame

Step 4
cut basket
rungs

Step 2
drill

Step 3
cut foot

Step 2
drill

71

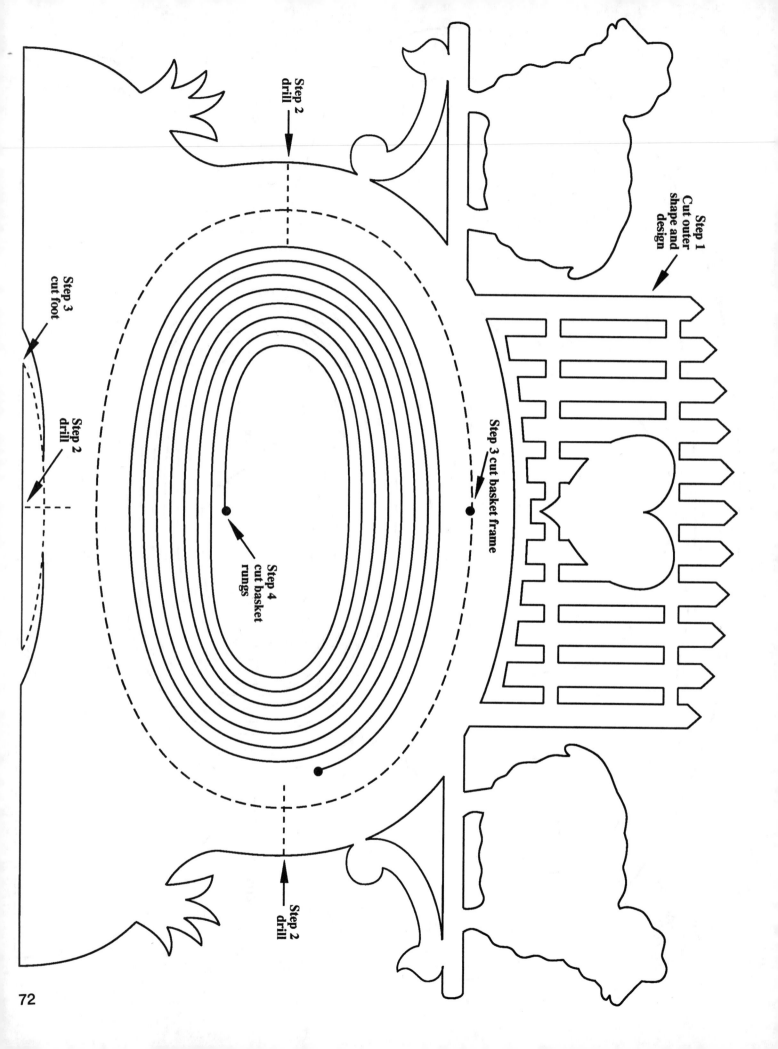

Step 1
Cut outer
shape and
design

Step 2
drill

Step 3
cut foot

Step 2
drill

Step 3 cut basket frame

Step 4
cut basket
rungs

Step 2
drill

72

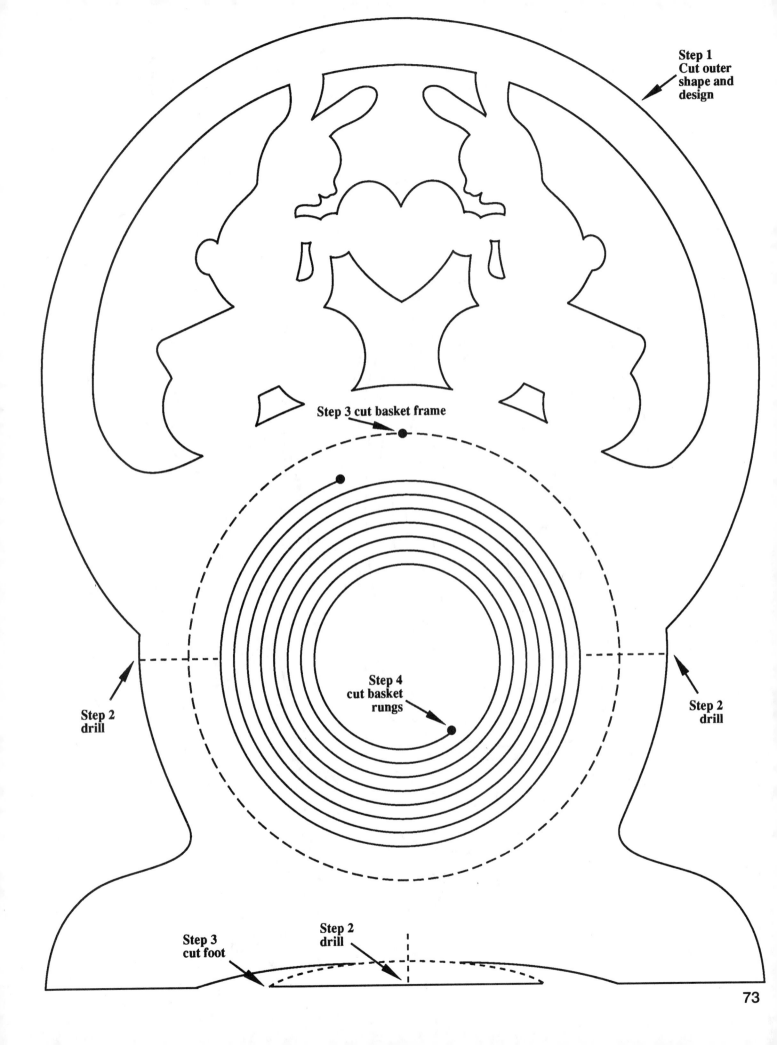

Step 1
Cut outer
shape and
design

Step 3 cut basket frame

Step 2
drill

Step 4
cut basket
rungs

Step 2
drill

Step 3
cut foot

Step 2
drill

73

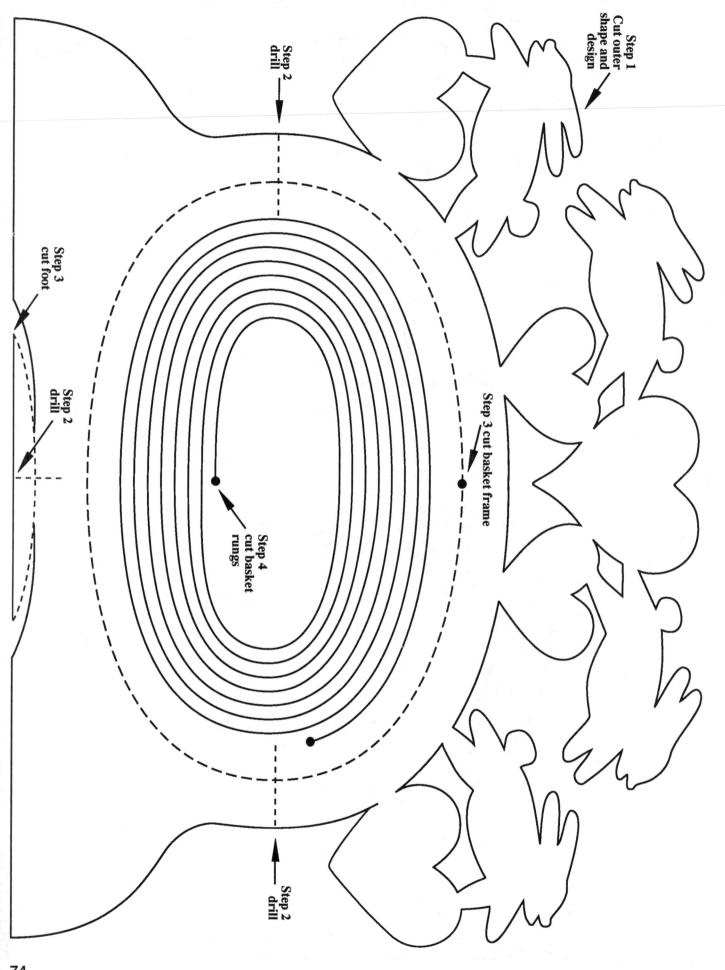

Step 1
Cut outer
shape and
design

Step 2
drill

Step 3
cut foot

Step 2
drill

Step 3 cut basket frame

Step 4
cut basket
rungs

Step 2
drill

74

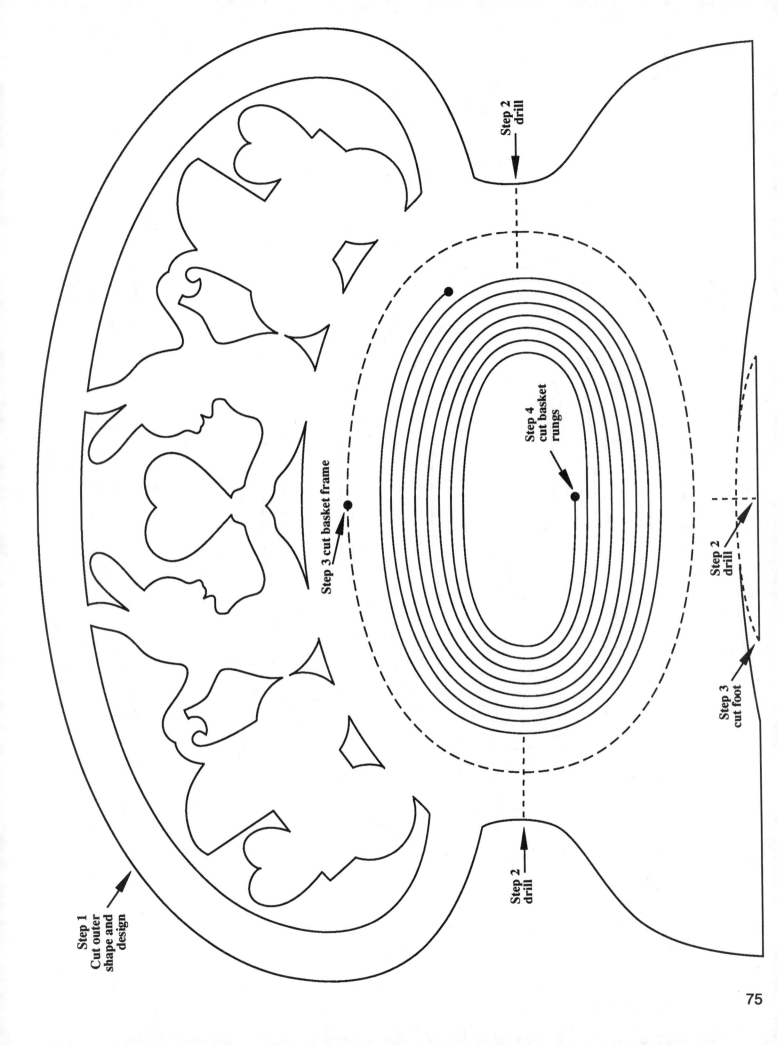

Step 2
drill

Step 4
cut basket
rungs

Step 3 cut basket frame

Step 2
drill

Step 3
cut foot

Step 2
drill

Step 1
Cut outer
shape and
design

75

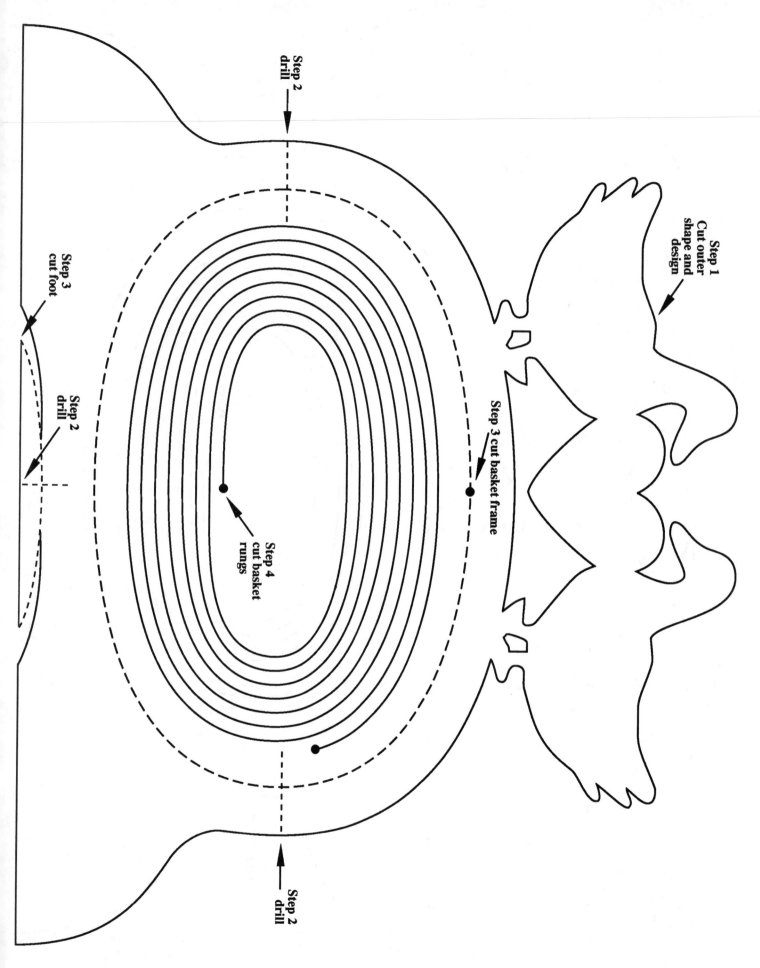

Step 1
Cut outer
shape and
design

Step 3 cut basket frame

Step 2
drill

Step 2
drill

Step 4
cut basket
rungs

Step 3
cut foot

Step 2
drill

Step 2
drill

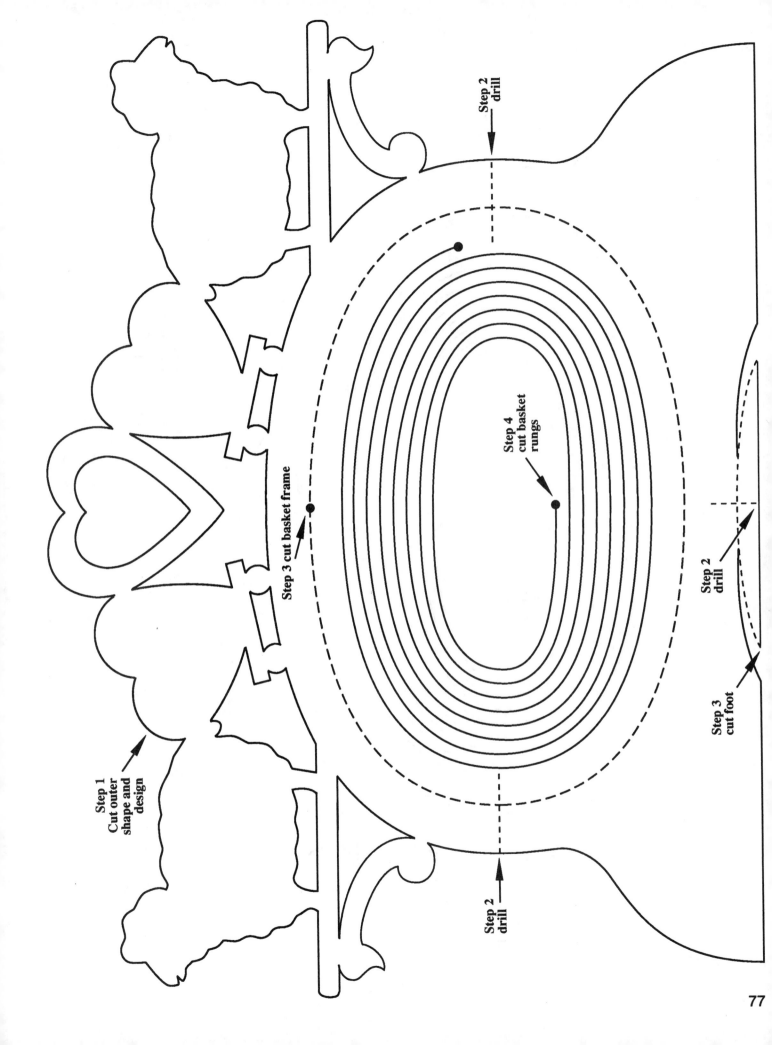

Step 1
Cut outer
shape and
design

Step 3 cut basket frame

Step 2
drill

Step 4
cut basket
rungs

Step 2
drill

Step 2
drill

Step 3
cut foot

77

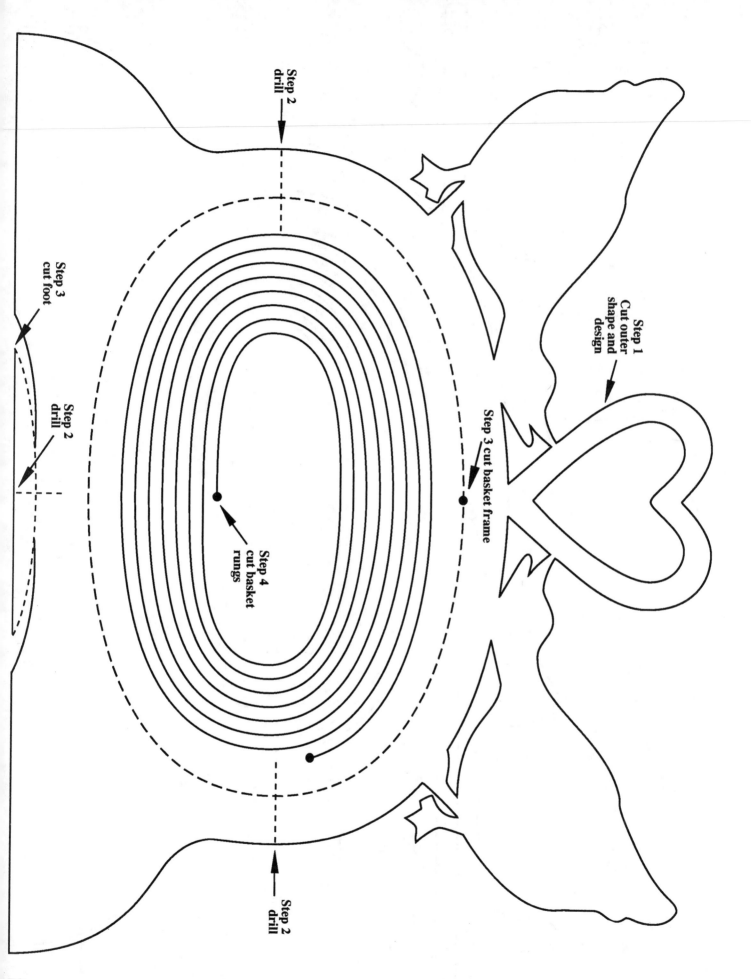

Step 2
drill

Step 1
Cut outer
shape and
design

Step 3
cut foot

Step 2
drill

Step 3 cut basket frame

Step 4
cut basket
rungs

Step 2
drill

78

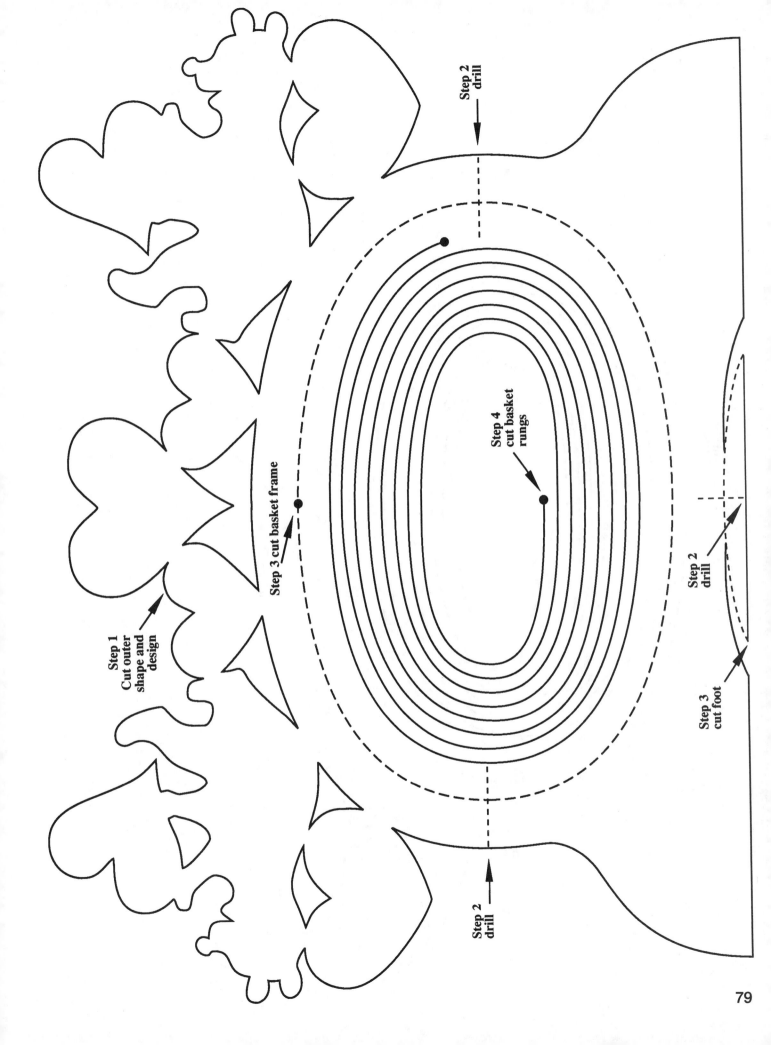

Step 2
drill

Step 4
cut basket
rungs

Step 3 cut basket frame

Step 1
Cut outer
shape and
design

Step 2
drill

Step 2
drill

Step 3
cut foot

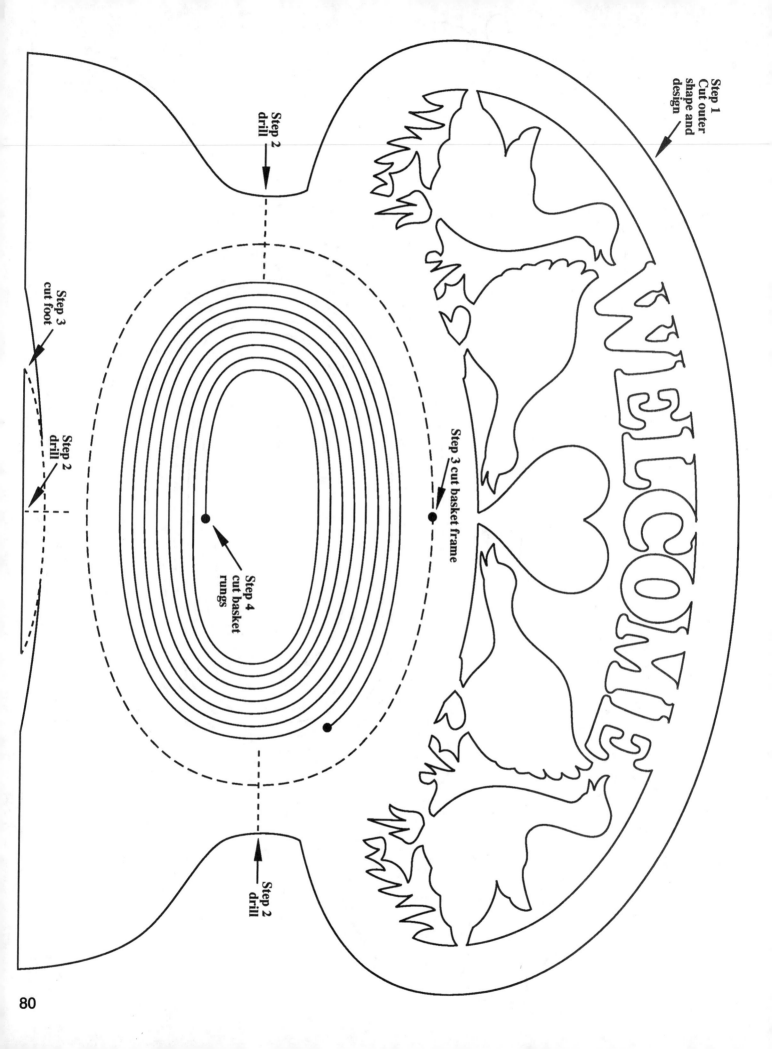

Step 1
Cut outer
shape and
design

Step 2
drill

Step 3
cut foot

Step 2
drill

Step 3 cut basket frame

Step 4
cut basket
rungs

Step 2
drill

WELCOME

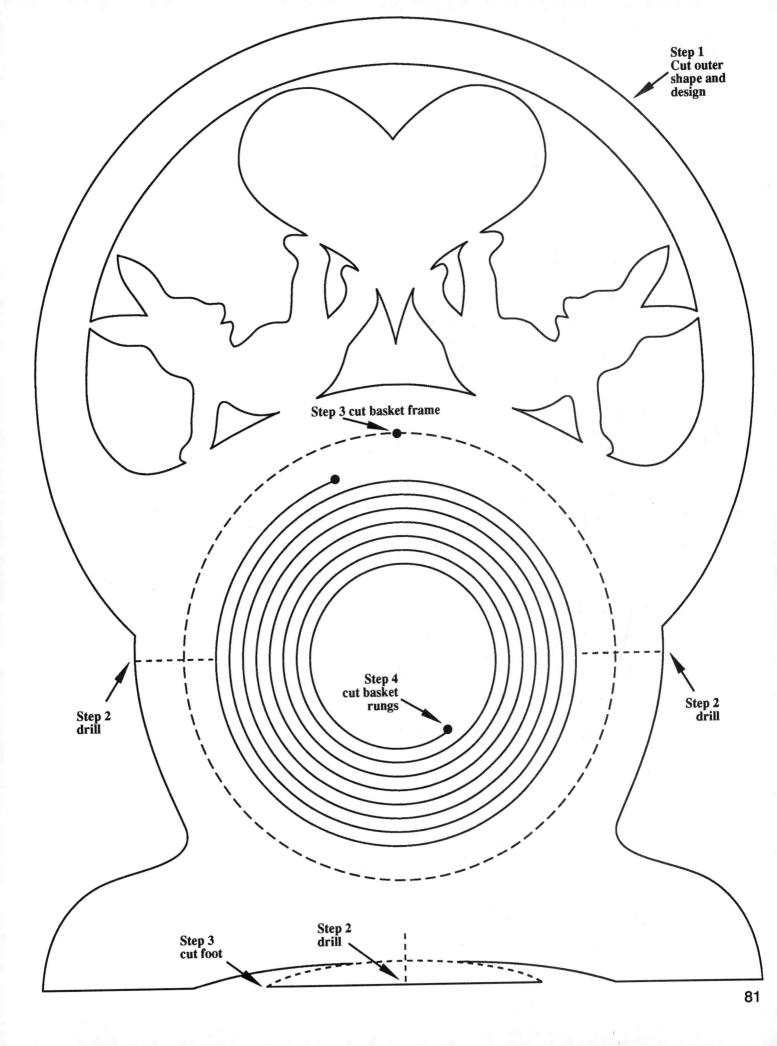

Step 1
Cut outer
shape and
design

Step 3 cut basket frame

Step 2
drill

Step 2
drill

Step 4
cut basket
rungs

Step 3
cut foot

Step 2
drill

81

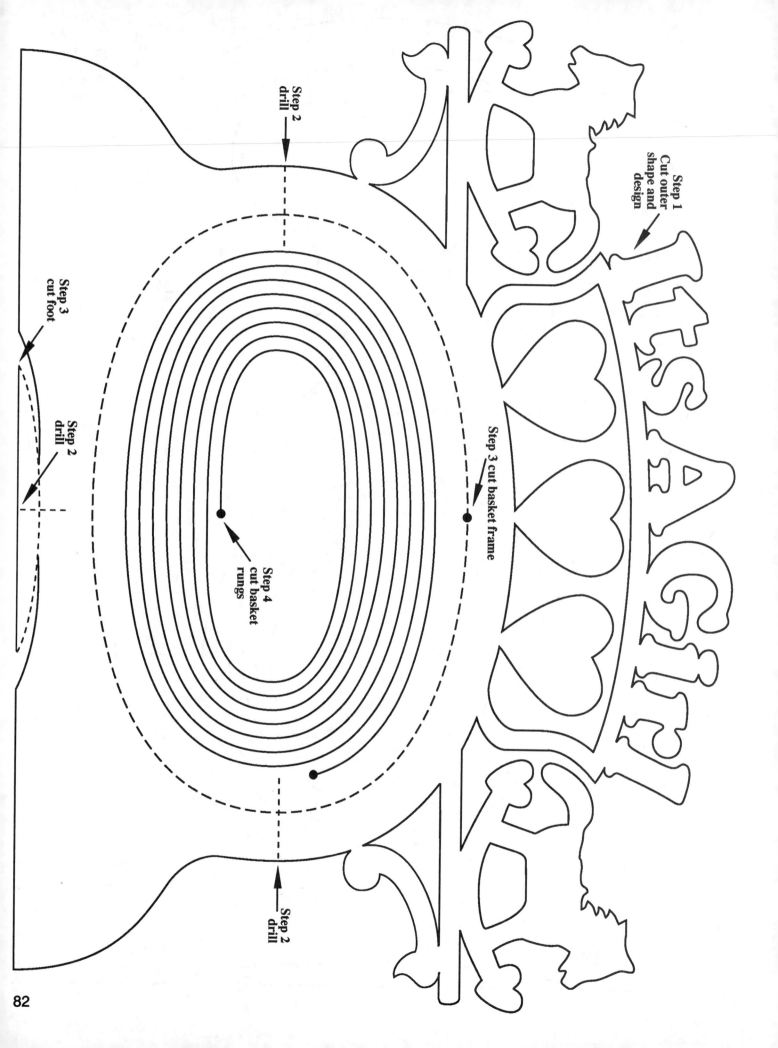

Step 1
Cut outer
shape and
design

Step 2
drill

Step 3
cut foot

Step 2
drill

Step 3 cut basket frame

Step 4
cut basket
rungs

Step 2
drill

It's A Girl!

82

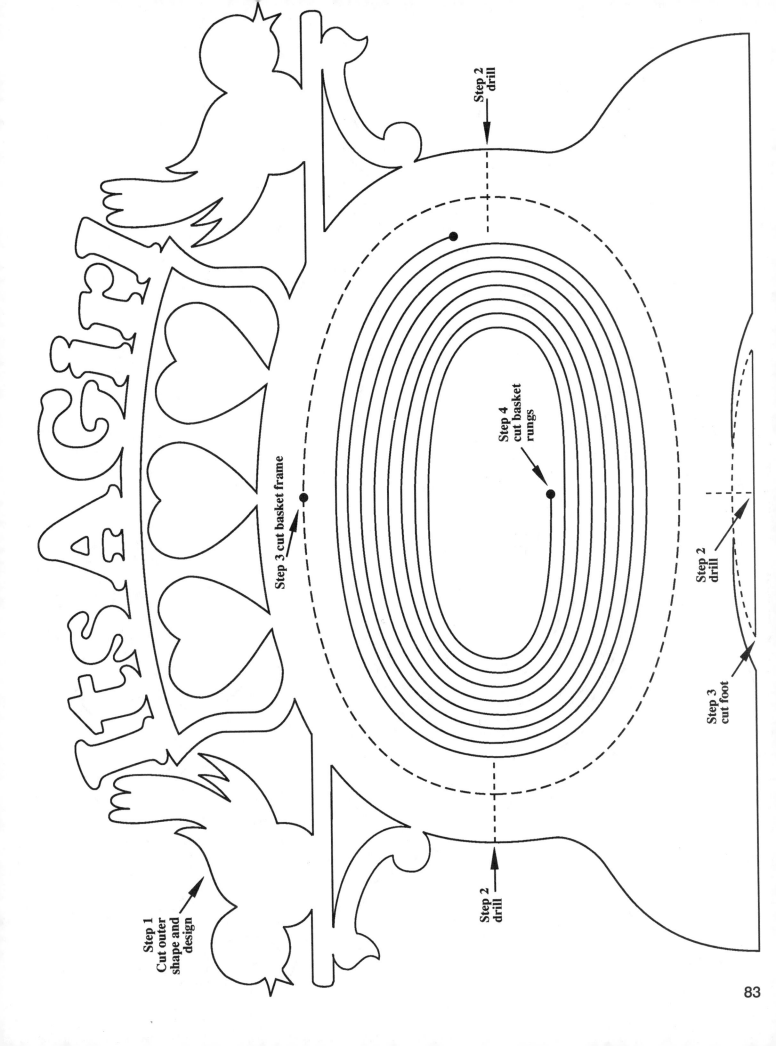

It's A Girl

Step 1
Cut outer
shape and
design

Step 3 cut basket frame

Step 2
drill

Step 2
drill

Step 2
drill

Step 4
cut basket
rungs

Step 3
cut foot

83

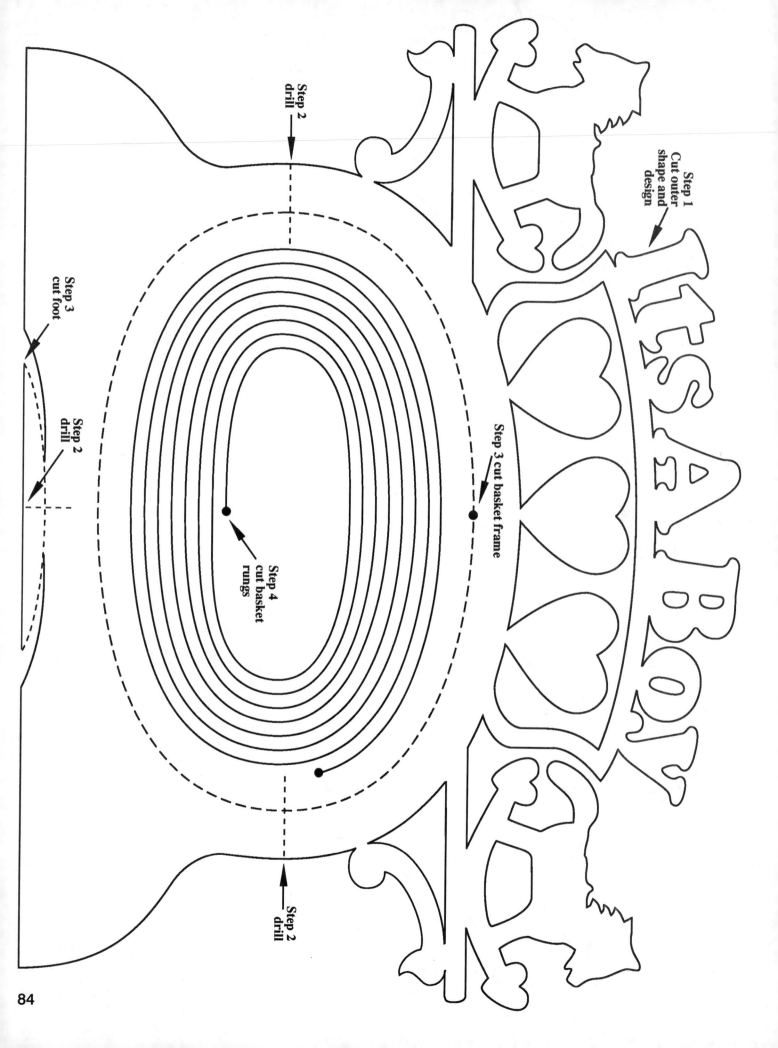

Step 1
Cut outer
shape and
design

Step 2
drill

Step 3
cut foot

Step 2
drill

Step 3 cut basket frame

Step 4
cut basket
rungs

Step 2
drill

84

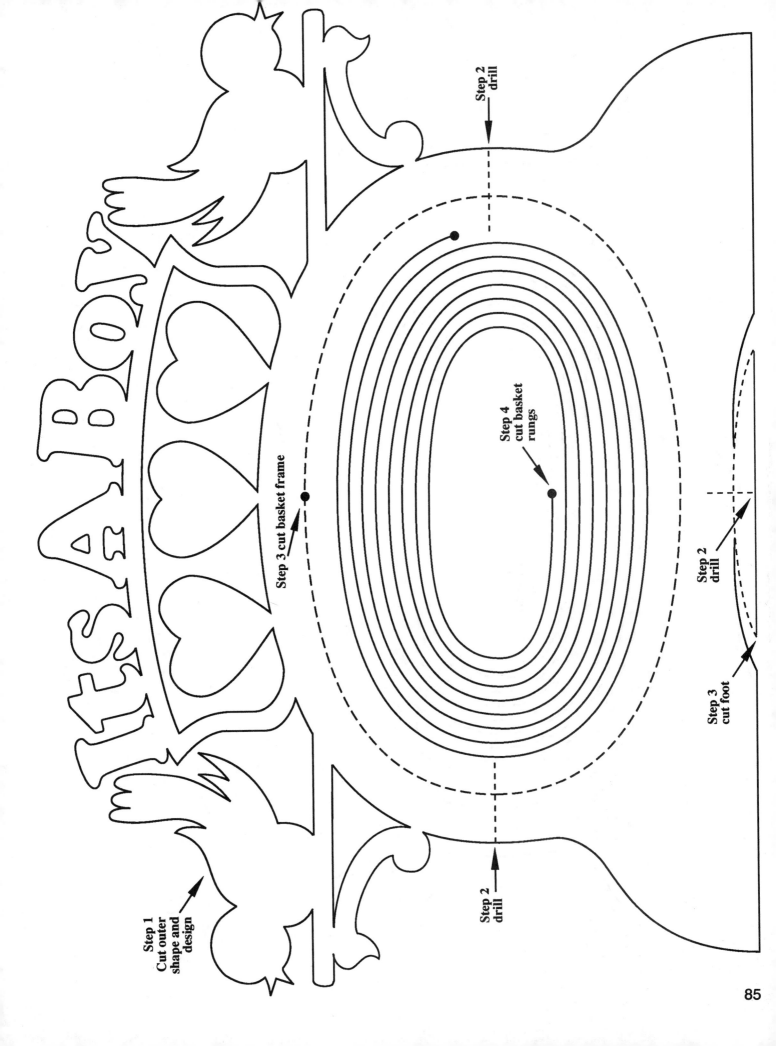

It's A Boy

Step 1
Cut outer
shape and
design

Step 3 cut basket frame

Step 2
drill

Step 4
cut basket
rungs

Step 2
drill

Step 2
drill

Step 3
cut foot

85

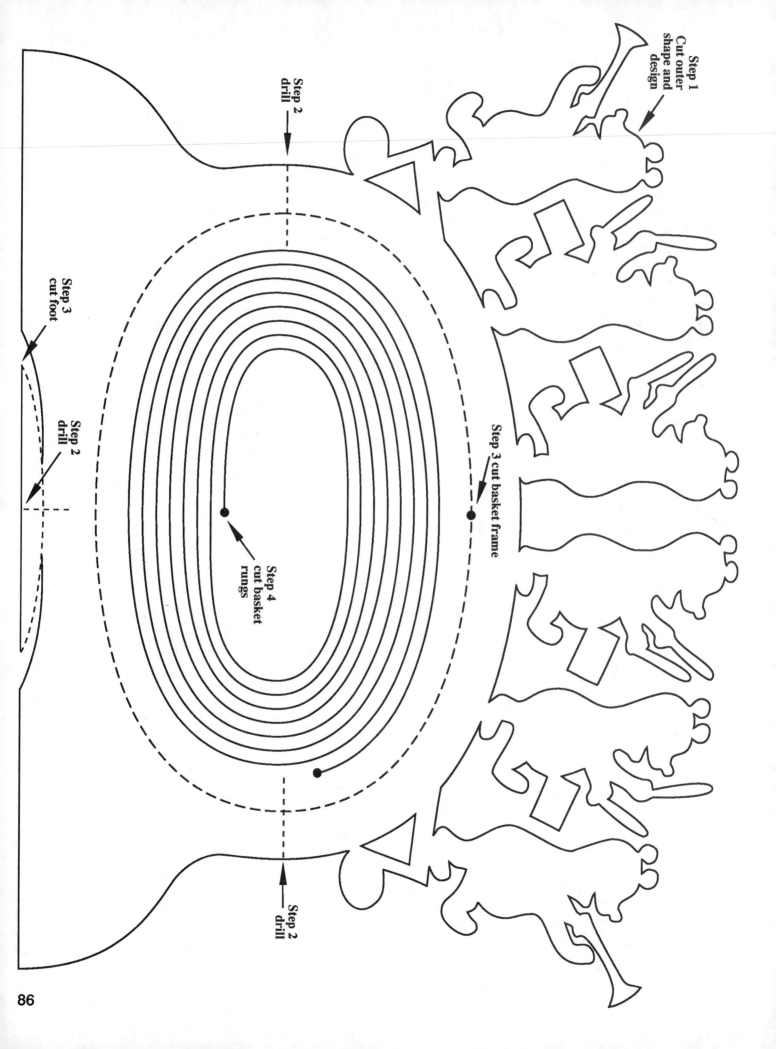

Step 1
Cut outer
shape and
design

Step 2
drill

Step 3
cut foot

Step 2
drill

Step 3 cut basket frame

Step 4
cut basket
rungs

Step 2
drill

86

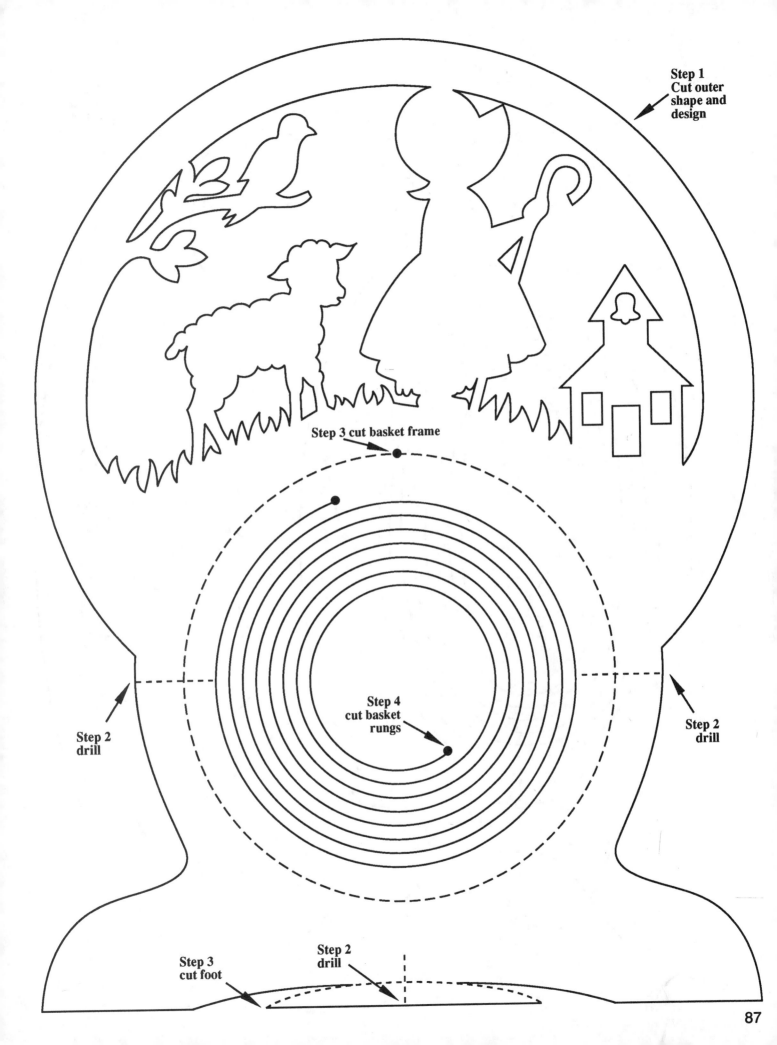

Step 1
Cut outer
shape and
design

Step 3 cut basket frame

Step 2
drill

Step 4
cut basket
rungs

Step 2
drill

Step 3
cut foot

Step 2
drill

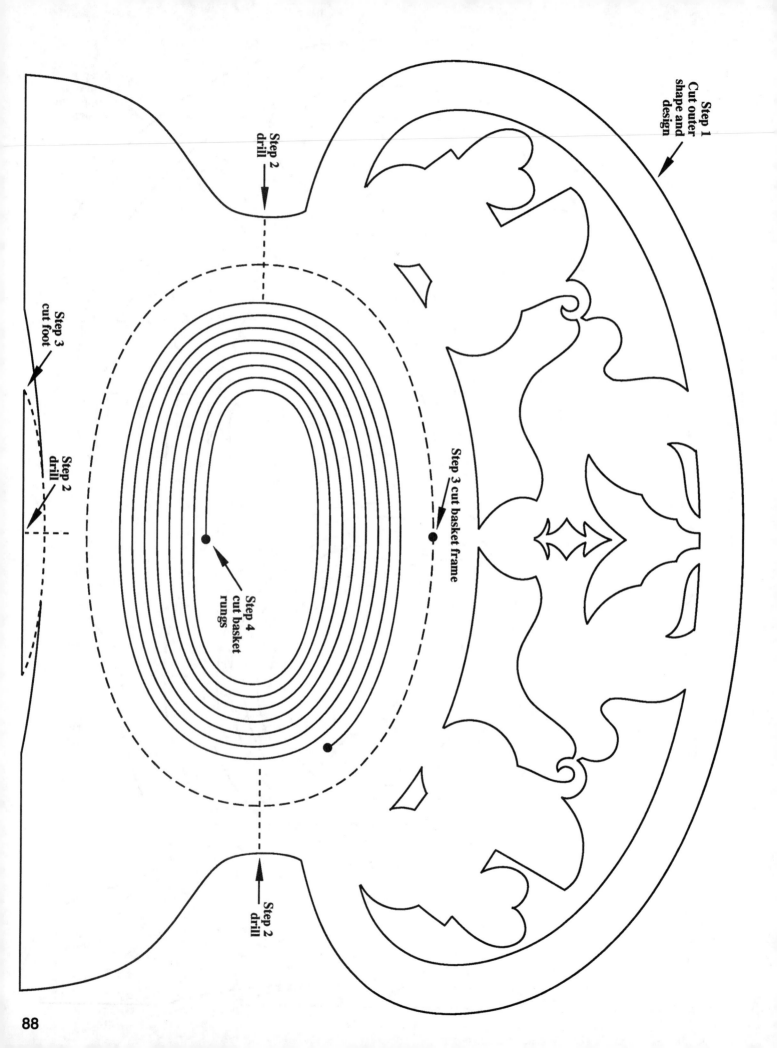

Step 1
Cut outer
shape and
design

Step 2
drill

Step 3
cut foot

Step 2
drill

Step 3 cut basket frame

Step 4
cut basket
rungs

Step 2
drill

88

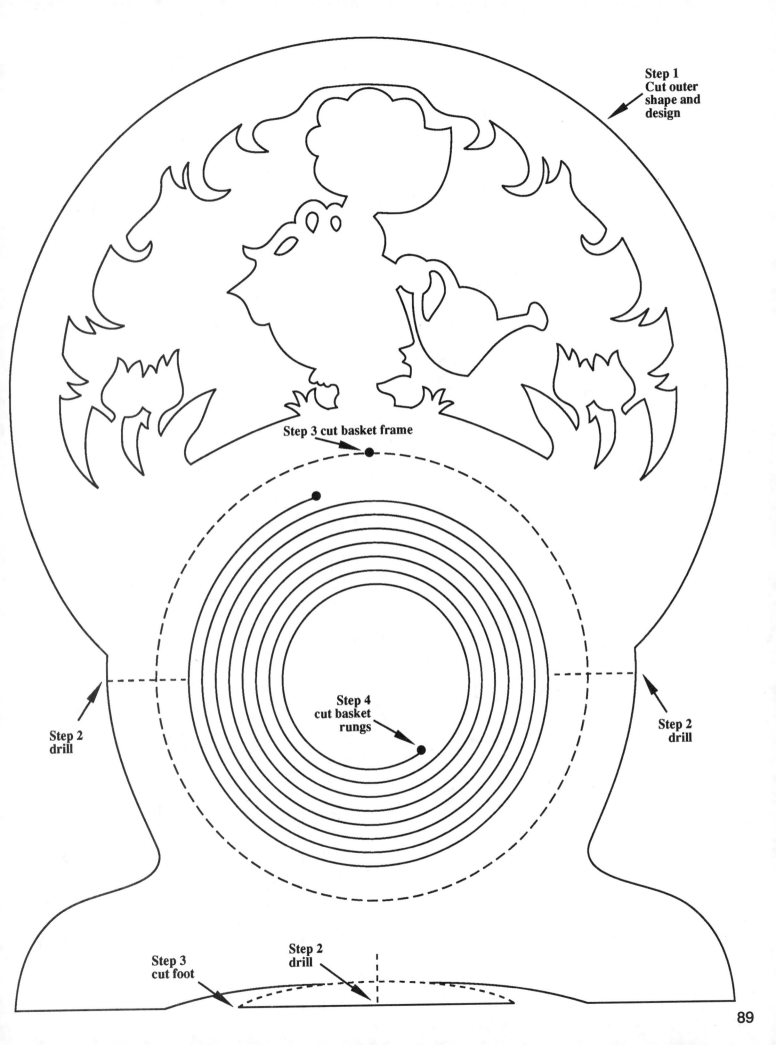

Step 1
Cut outer
shape and
design

Step 3 cut basket frame

Step 2
drill

Step 2
drill

Step 4
cut basket
rungs

Step 3
cut foot

Step 2
drill

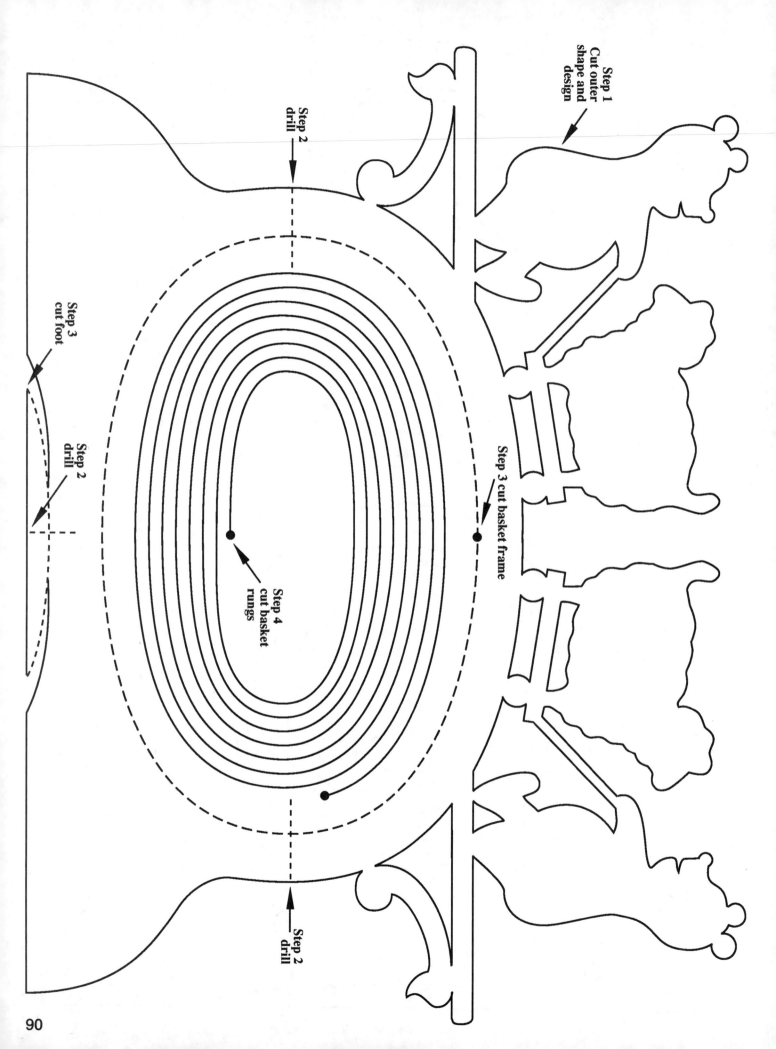

Step 1
Cut outer
shape and
design

Step 2
drill

Step 3
cut foot

Step 2
drill

Step 3 cut basket frame

Step 4
cut basket
rungs

Step 2
drill

90

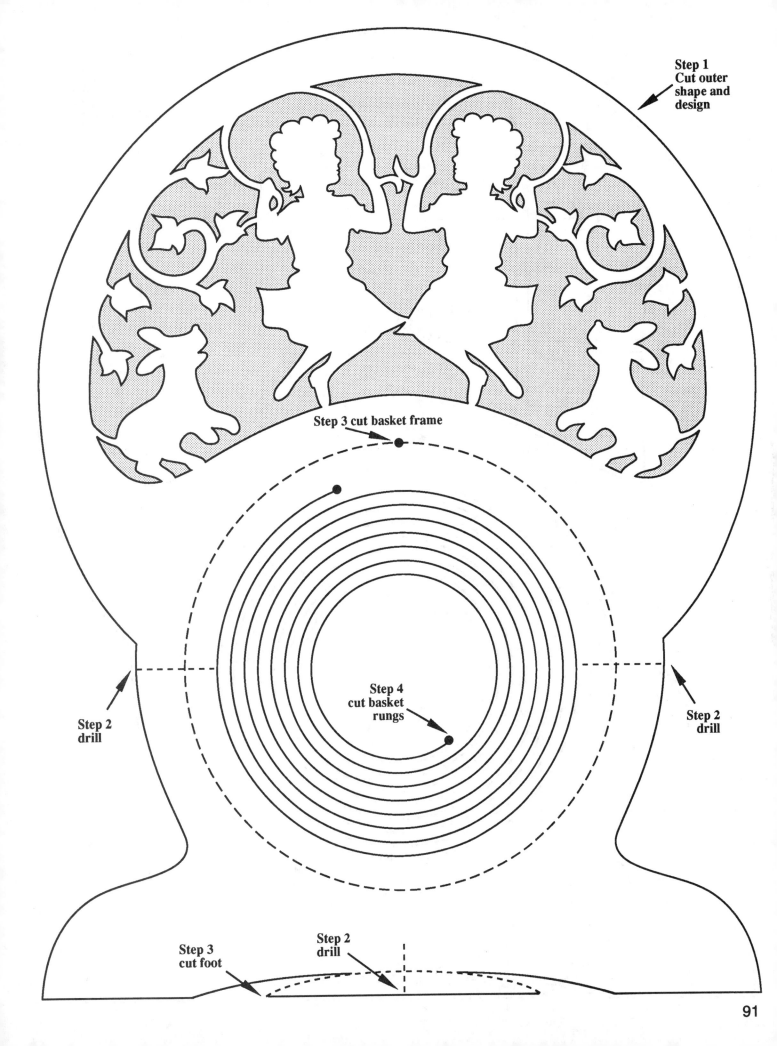

Step 1
Cut outer
shape and
design

Step 3 cut basket frame

Step 2
drill

Step 4
cut basket
rungs

Step 2
drill

Step 3
cut foot

Step 2
drill

91

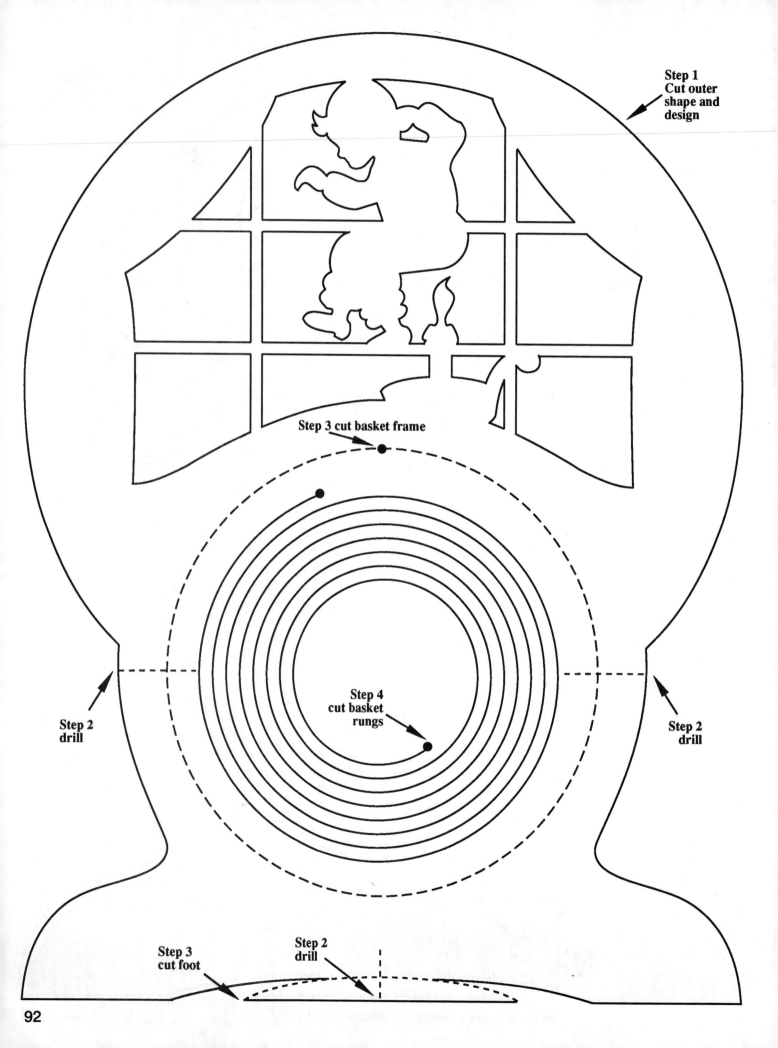

Step 1
Cut outer
shape and
design

Step 3 cut basket frame

Step 4
cut basket
rungs

Step 2
drill

Step 2
drill

Step 3
cut foot

Step 2
drill

92

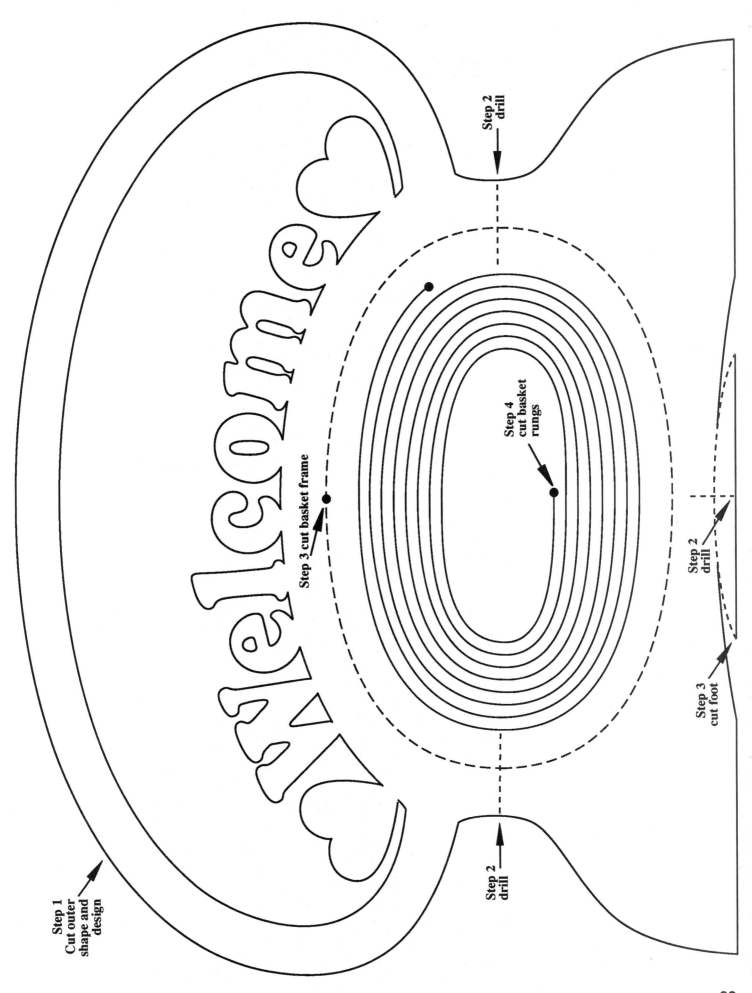

Step 1
Cut outer
shape and
design

Step 2
drill

Step 3 cut basket frame

Step 4
cut basket
rungs

Step 2
drill

Step 2
drill

Step 3
cut foot

99

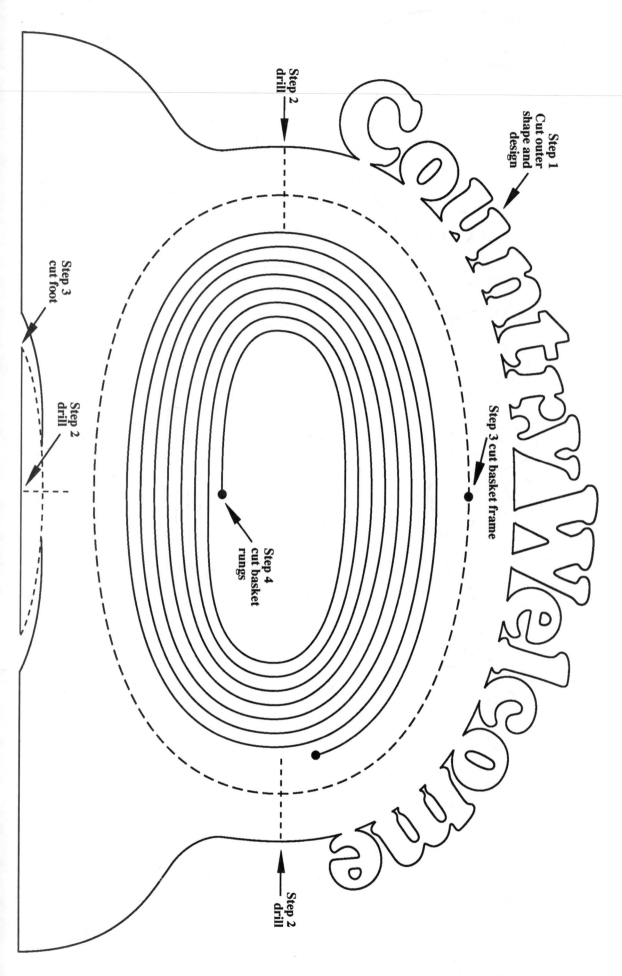

Step 2
drill

Step 1
Cut outer
shape and
design

Step 3
cut foot

Step 2
drill

Step 4
cut basket
rungs

Step 3 cut basket frame

Step 2
drill

CountryWelcome

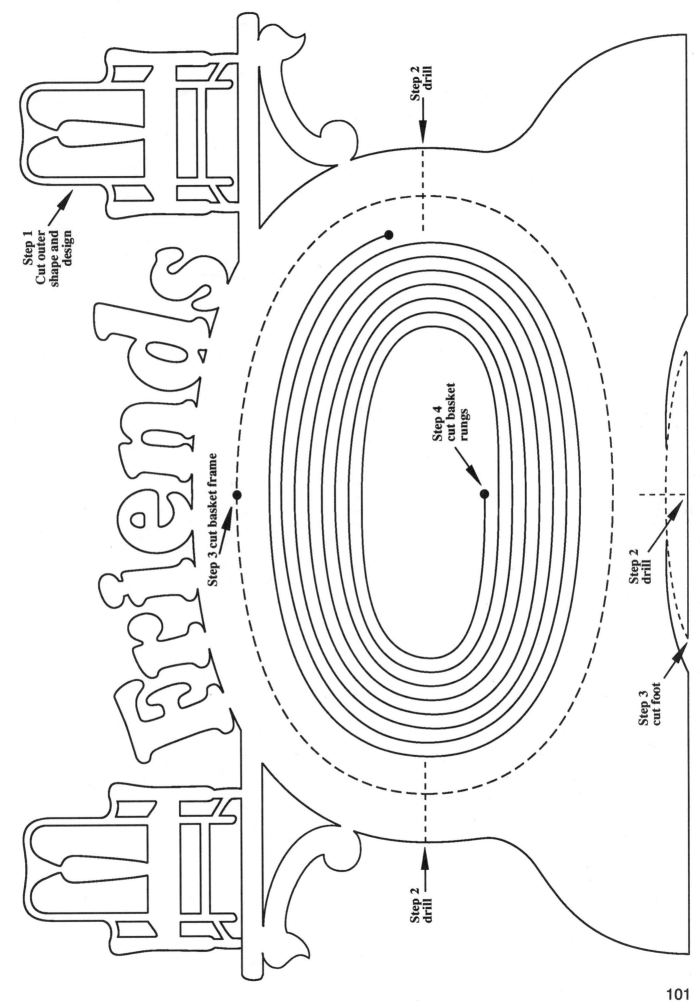

Step 1
Cut outer
shape and
design

Step 3 cut basket frame

Step 2
drill

Step 4
cut basket
rungs

Step 2
drill

Step 2
drill

Step 3
cut foot

101

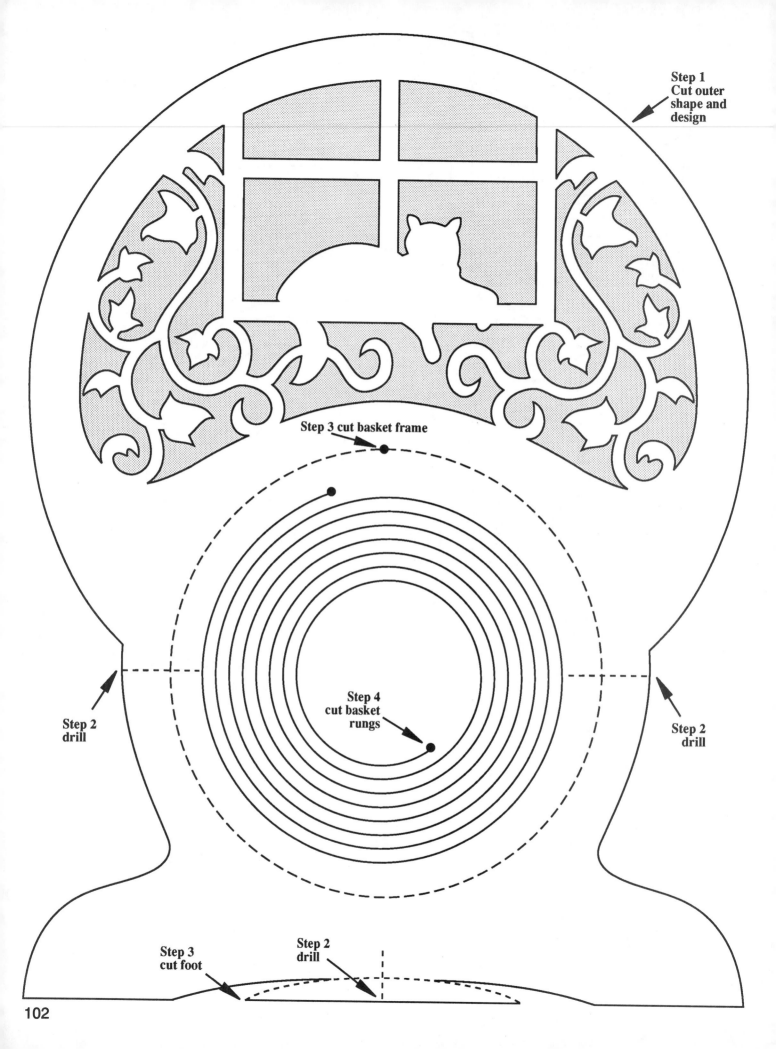

Step 1
Cut outer
shape and
design

Step 3 cut basket frame

Step 2
drill

Step 2
drill

Step 4
cut basket
rungs

Step 3
cut foot

Step 2
drill

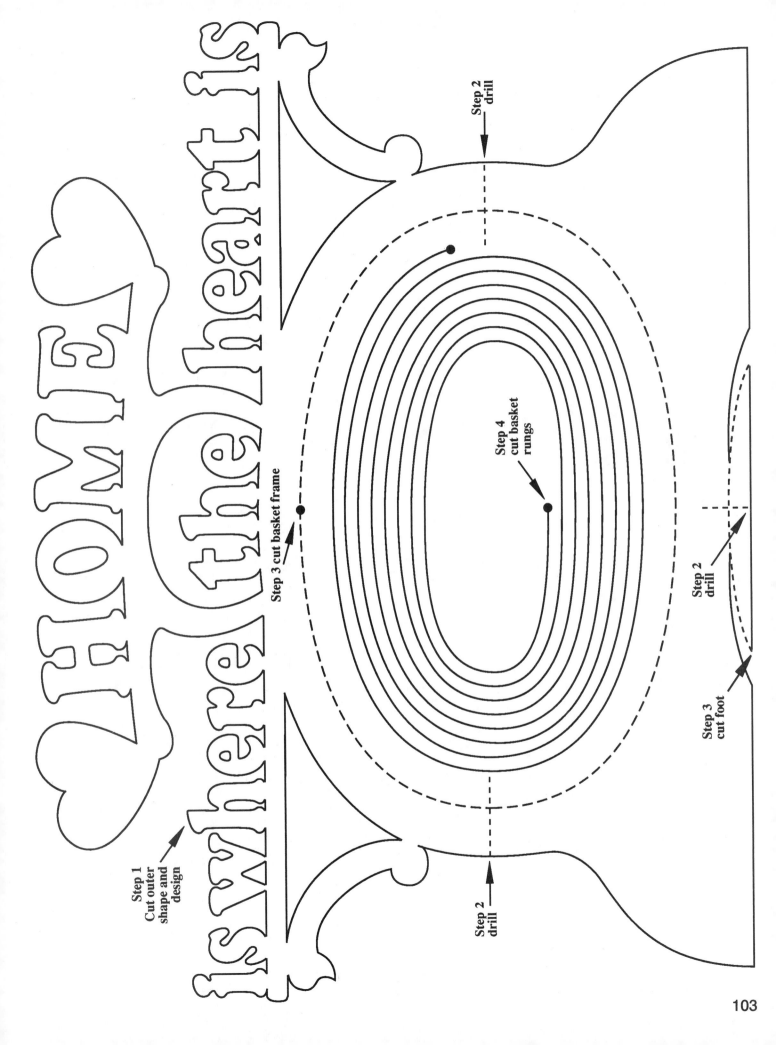

HOME is where the heart is

Step 1
Cut outer
shape and
design

Step 2
drill

Step 3 cut basket frame

Step 4
cut basket
rungs

Step 2
drill

Step 2
drill

Step 3
cut foot

103

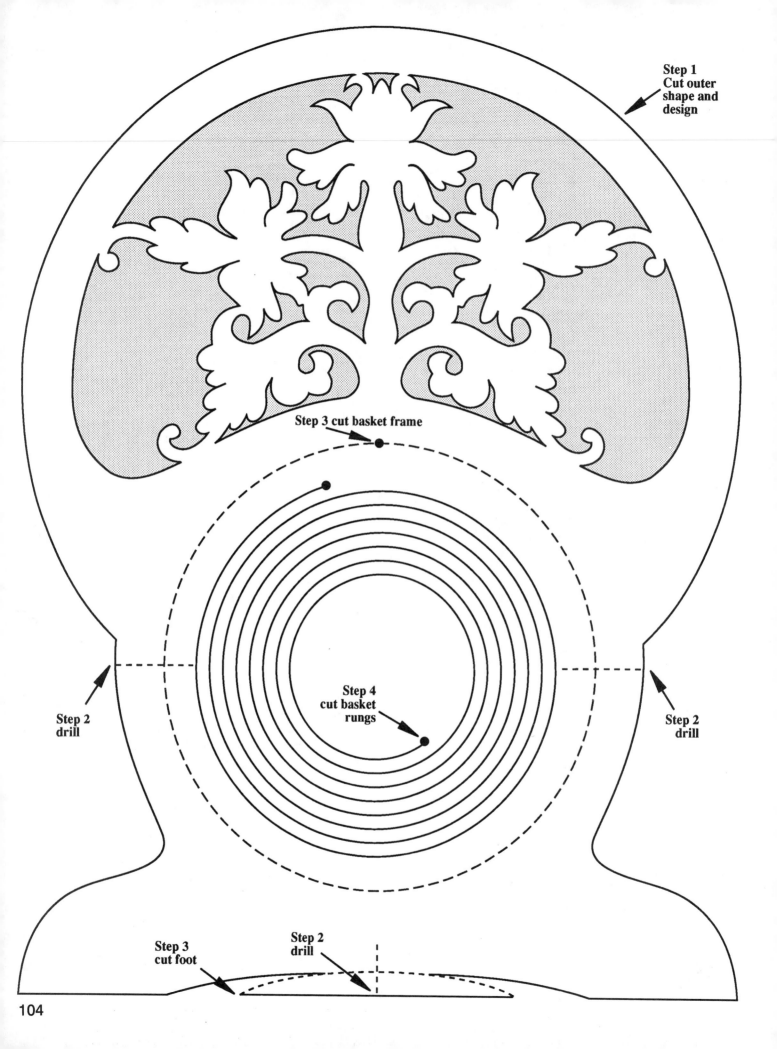

Step 1
Cut outer
shape and
design

Step 3 cut basket frame

Step 2
drill

Step 4
cut basket
rungs

Step 2
drill

Step 3
cut foot

Step 2
drill

104

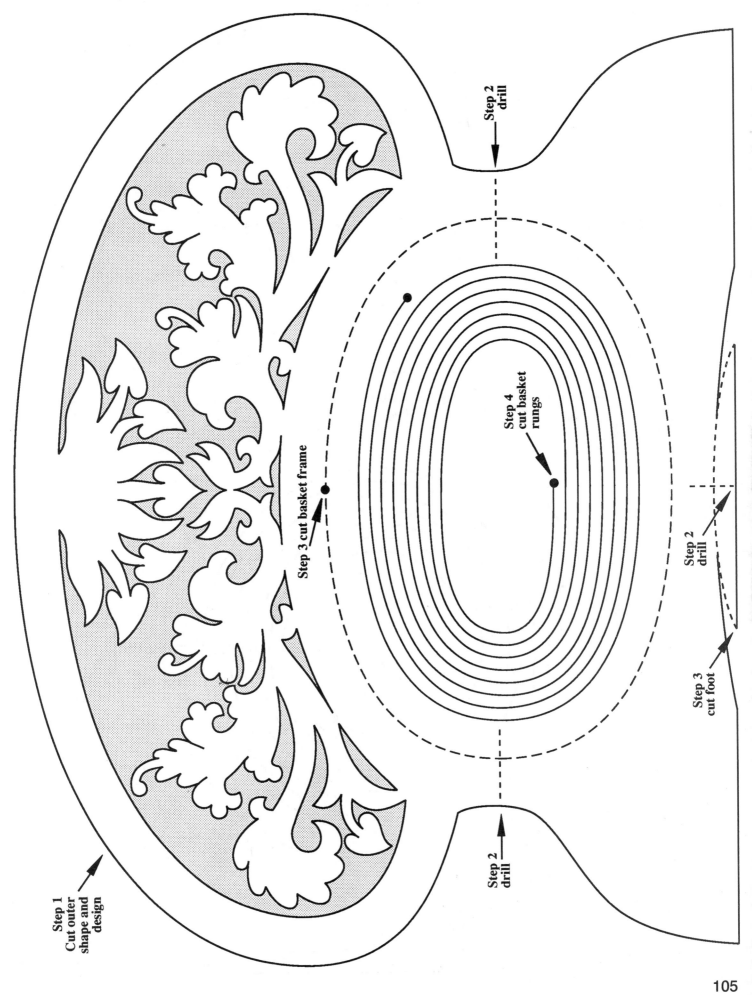

Step 2
drill

Step 4
cut basket
rungs

Step 2
drill

Step 3
cut foot

Step 3 cut basket frame

Step 2
drill

Step 1
Cut outer
shape and
design

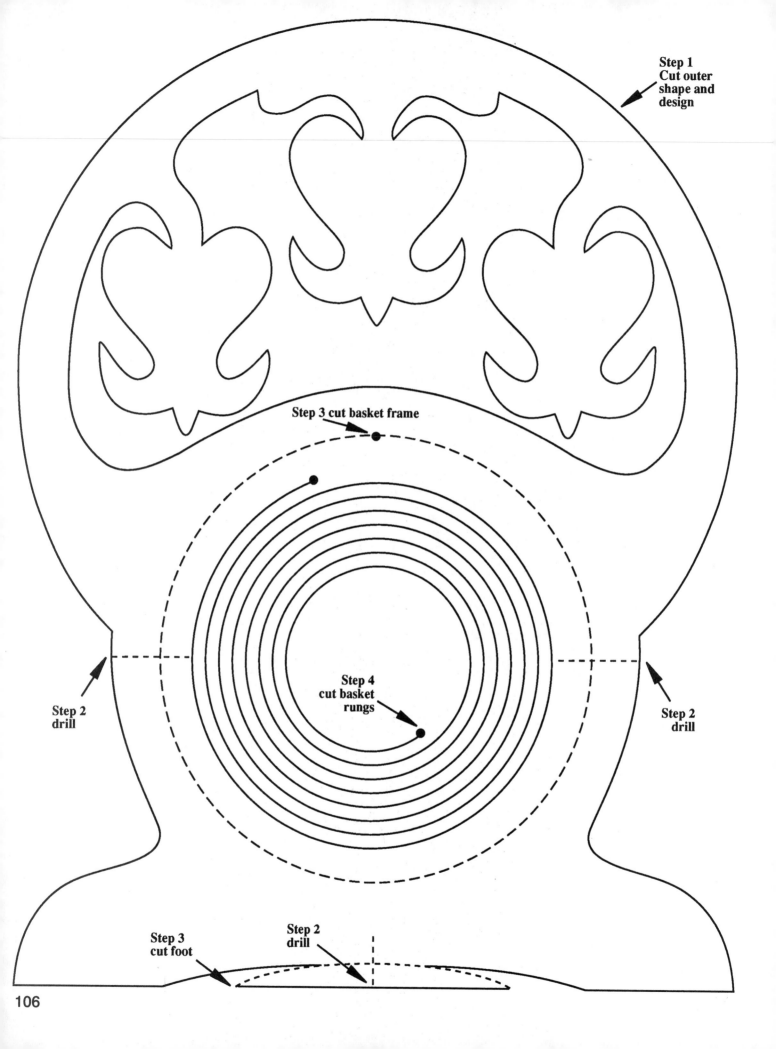

Step 1
Cut outer
shape and
design

Step 3 cut basket frame

Step 2
drill

Step 4
cut basket
rungs

Step 2
drill

Step 3
cut foot

Step 2
drill

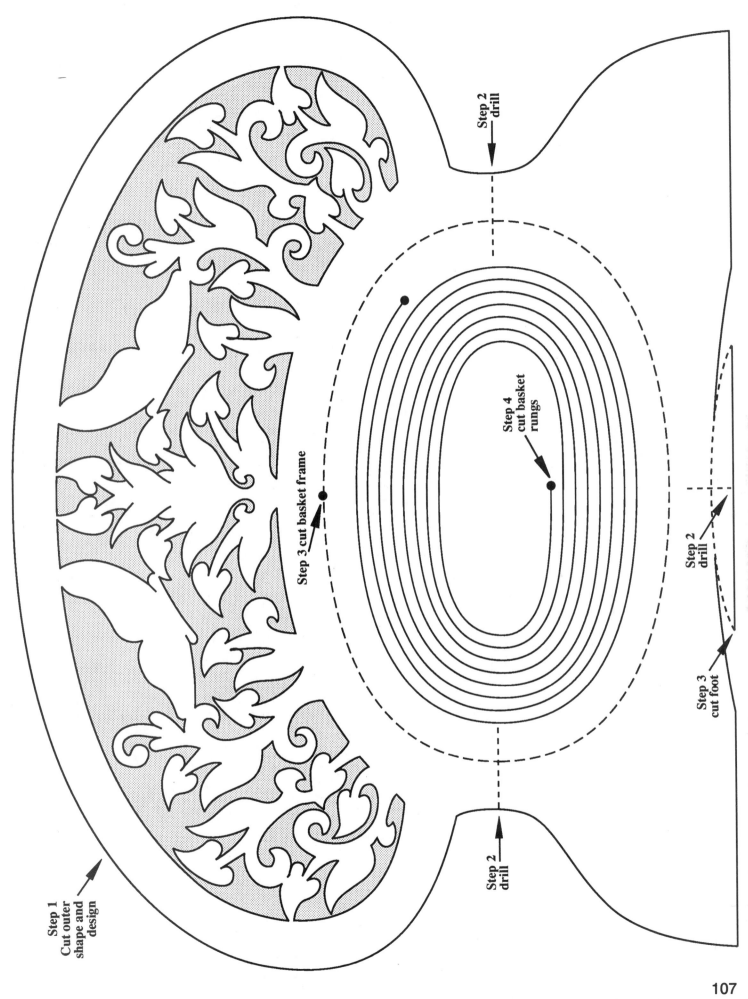

Step 1
Cut outer
shape and
design

Step 2
drill

Step 3 cut basket frame

Step 4
cut basket
rungs

Step 2
drill

Step 3
cut foot

Step 2
drill

107

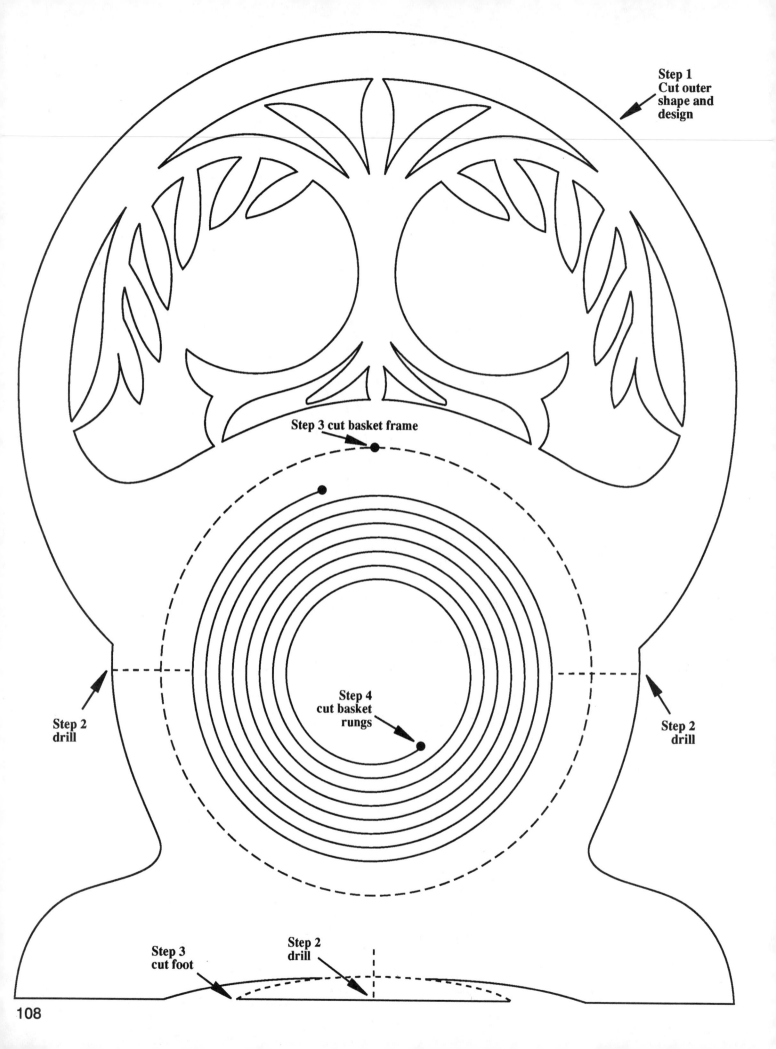

Step 1
Cut outer
shape and
design

Step 3 cut basket frame

Step 2
drill

Step 4
cut basket
rungs

Step 2
drill

Step 3
cut foot

Step 2
drill

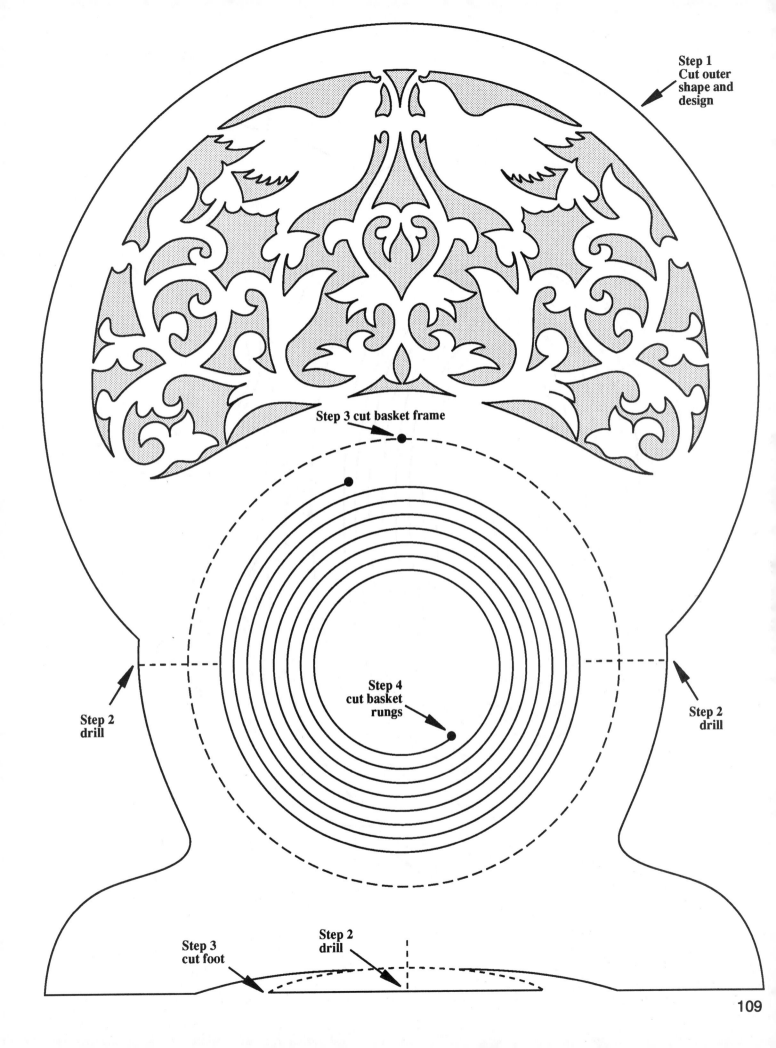

Step 1
Cut outer
shape and
design

Step 3 cut basket frame

Step 2
drill

Step 4
cut basket
rungs

Step 2
drill

Step 3
cut foot

Step 2
drill

109

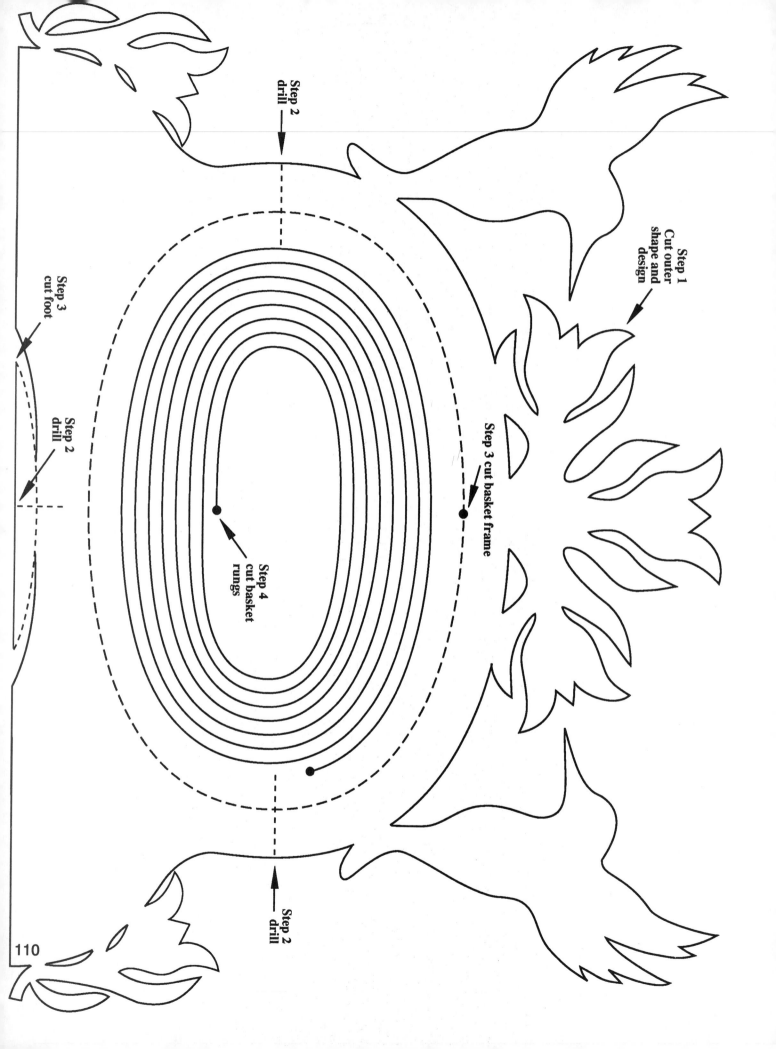

Step 1
Cut outer
shape and
design

Step 2
drill

Step 3
cut foot

Step 2
drill

Step 3 cut basket frame

Step 4
cut basket
rungs

Step 2
drill

110

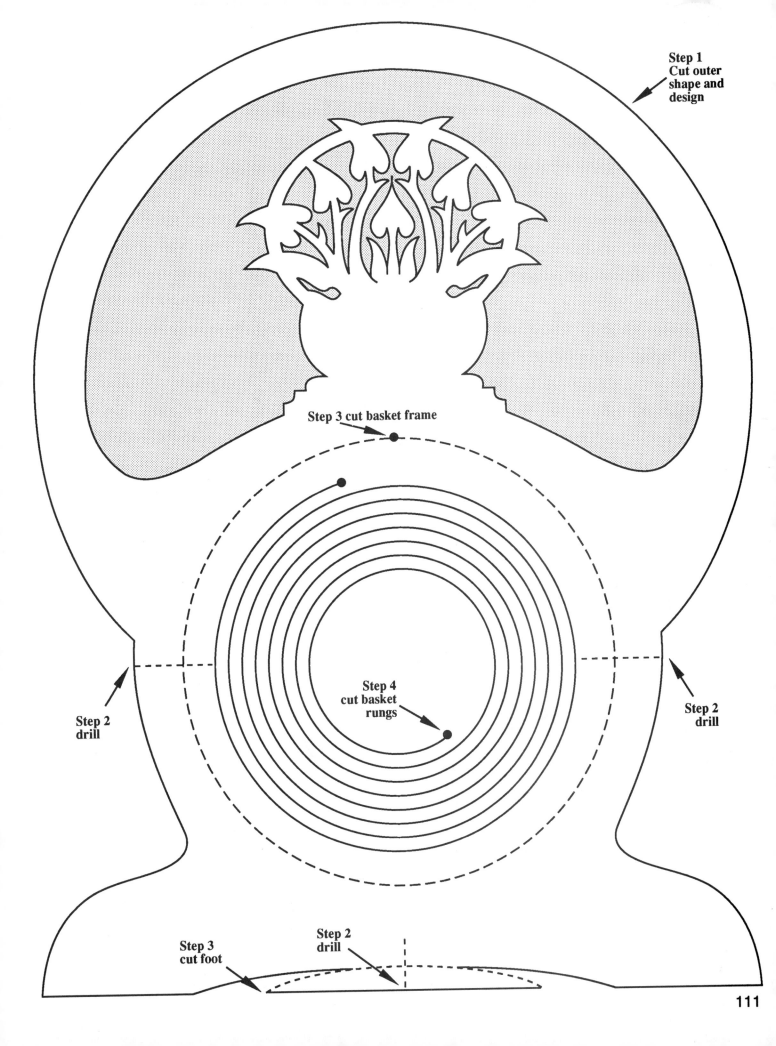

Step 1
Cut outer
shape and
design

Step 3 cut basket frame

Step 2
drill

Step 4
cut basket
rungs

Step 2
drill

Step 3
cut foot

Step 2
drill

111

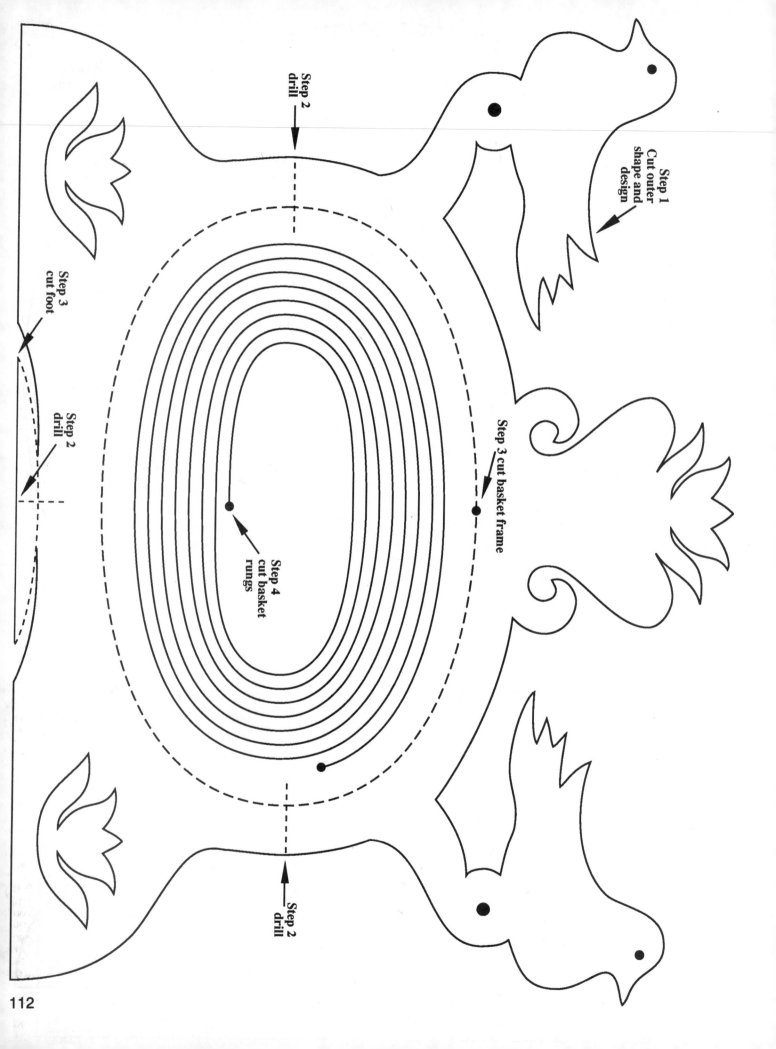

Step 2
drill

Step 1
Cut outer
shape and
design

Step 3
cut foot

Step 3 cut basket frame

Step 2
drill

Step 4
cut basket
rungs

Step 2
drill

112

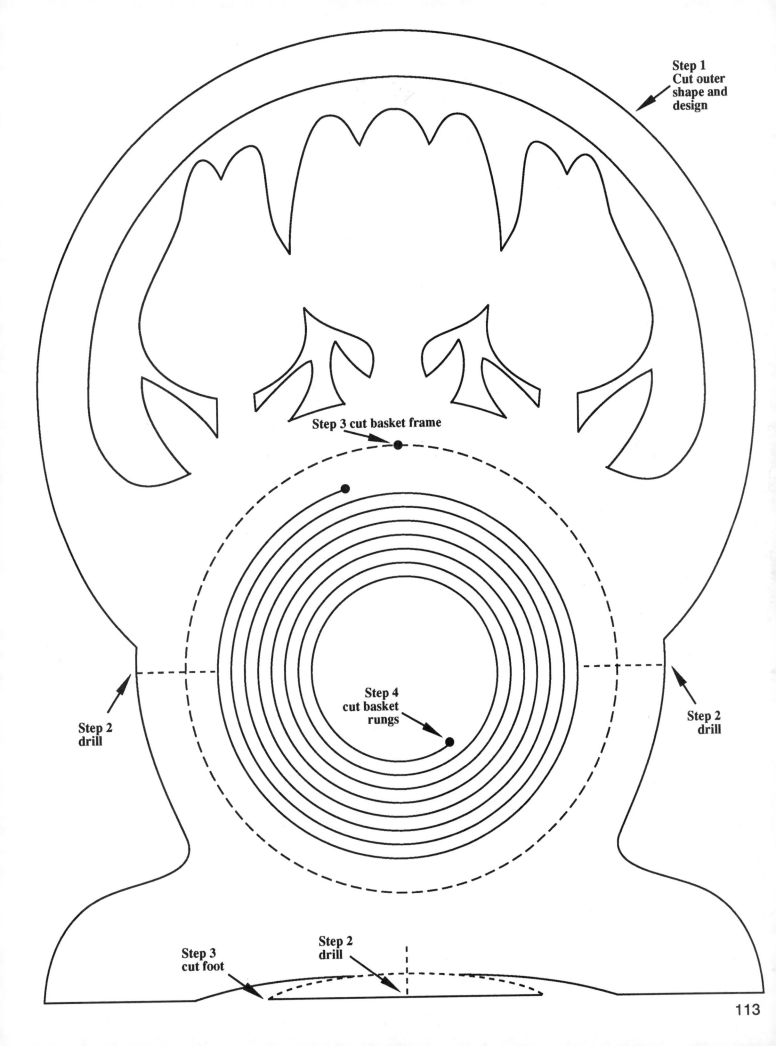

Step 1
Cut outer
shape and
design

Step 3 cut basket frame

Step 2
drill

Step 2
drill

Step 4
cut basket
rungs

Step 3
cut foot

Step 2
drill

113

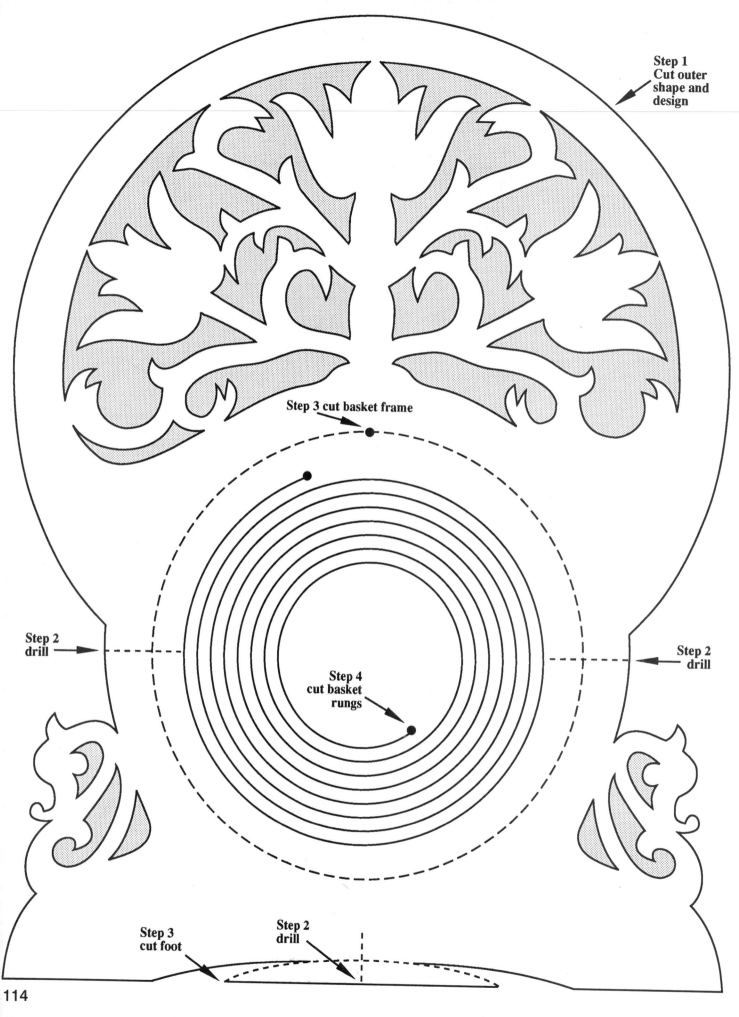

Step 1
Cut outer
shape and
design

Step 3 cut basket frame

Step 2
drill

Step 2
drill

Step 4
cut basket
rungs

Step 3
cut foot

Step 2
drill

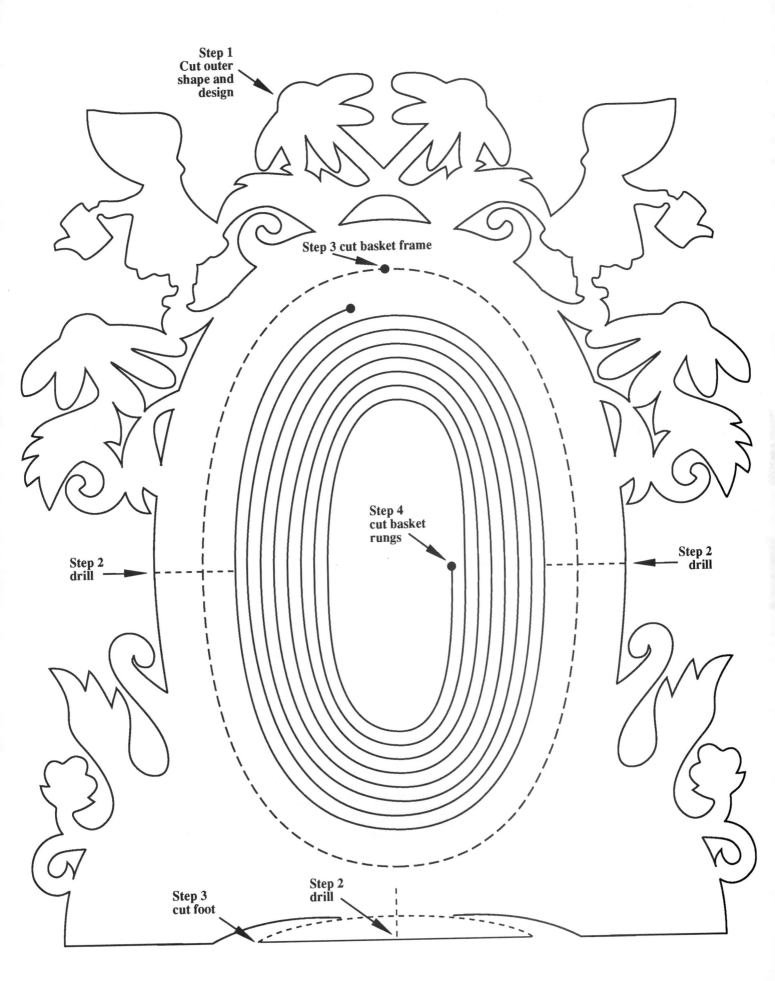

Step 1
Cut outer
shape and
design

Step 3 cut basket frame

Step 4
cut basket
rungs

Step 2
drill

Step 2
drill

Step 3
cut foot

Step 2
drill

115

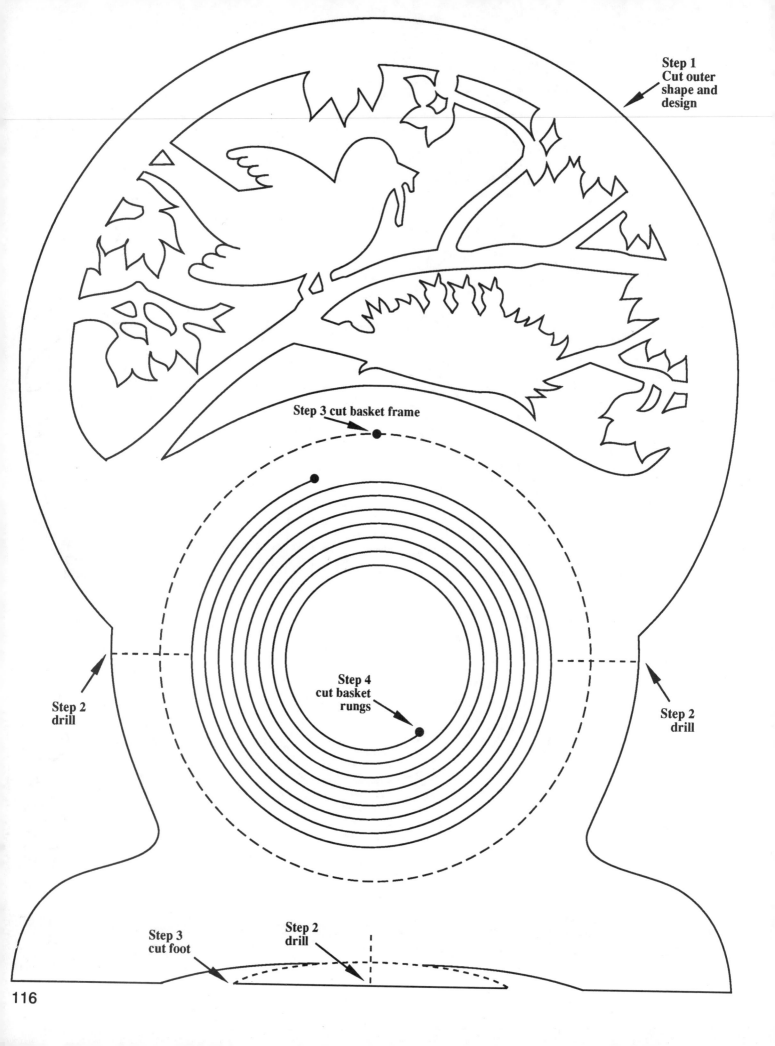

Step 1
Cut outer
shape and
design

Step 3 cut basket frame

Step 2
drill

Step 2
drill

Step 4
cut basket
rungs

Step 3
cut foot

Step 2
drill

116

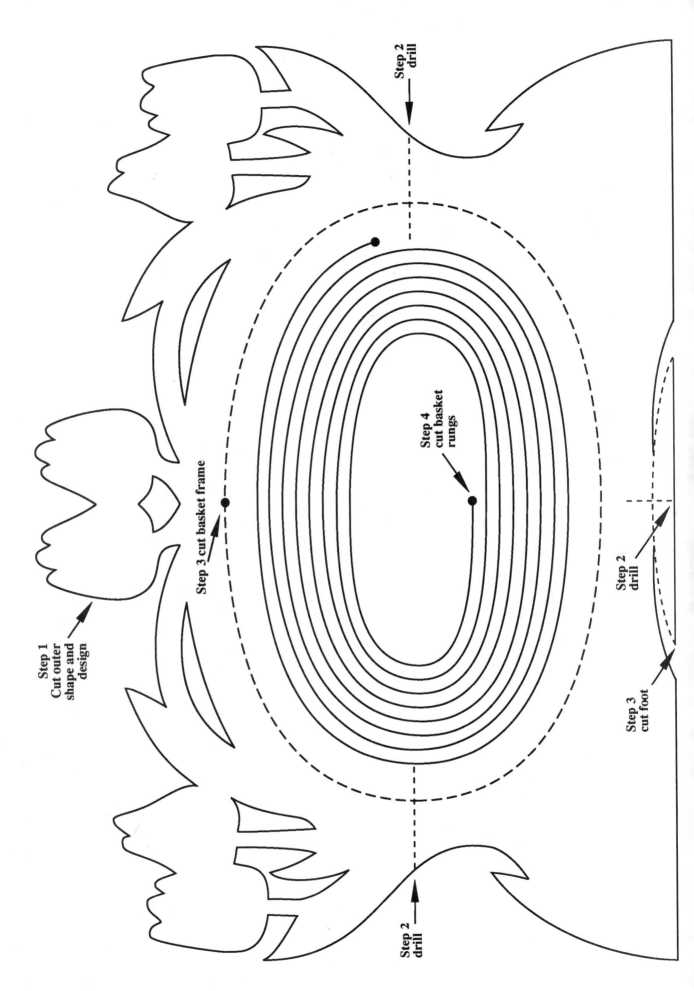

Step 2
drill

Step 1
Cut outer
shape and
design

Step 3 cut basket frame

Step 4
cut basket
rungs

Step 2
drill

Step 3
cut foot

Step 2
drill

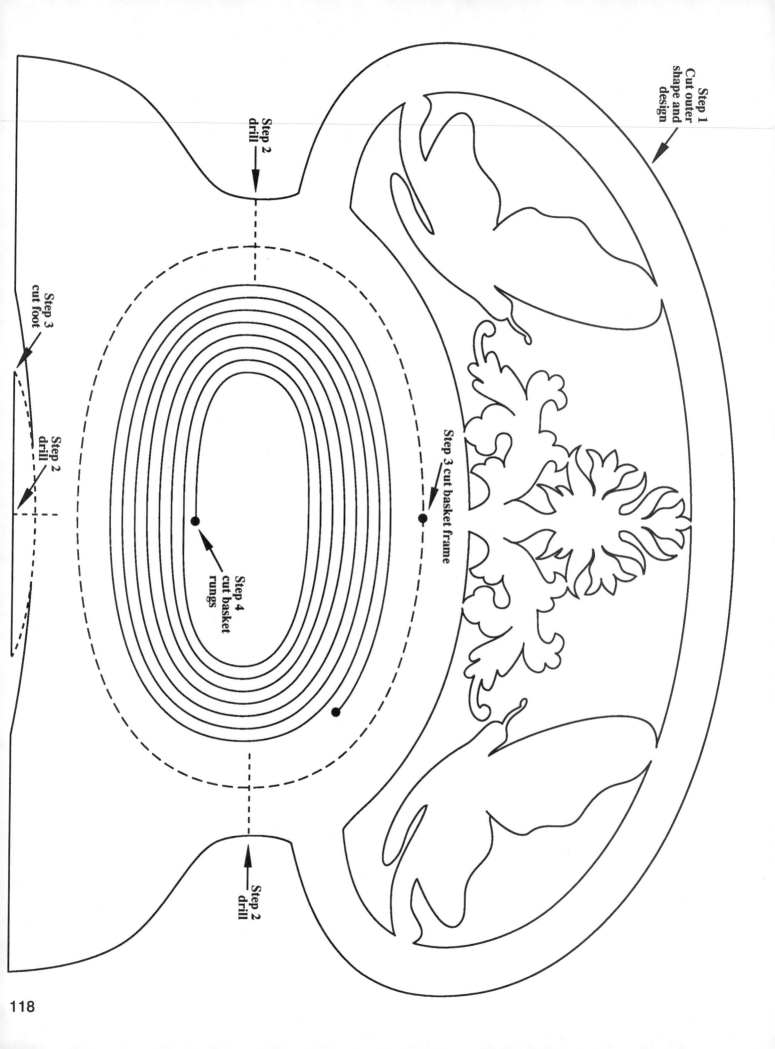

Step 1
Cut outer
shape and
design

Step 2
drill

Step 3
cut foot

Step 2
drill

Step 3 cut basket frame

Step 4
cut basket
rungs

Step 2
drill

118

FREE CATALOG OFFER

Are you interested in more unique designs?

Yes, please add my name to your mailing list for a catalog of more unique ideas.

NAME _____

ADDRESS _____

CITY _____ STATE _____ ZIP_____

THE BERRY BASKET • PO BOX 925-BK2 • CENTRALIA, WA 98531 • **1-800-206-9009**

Do you have friends who are interested in a catalog of unique ideas?

Yes, please add my friend to your mailing list and send them a catalog of unique ideas.

NAME _____

ADDRESS _____

CITY _____ STATE _____ ZIP_____

THE BERRY BASKET • PO BOX 925-BK2 • CENTRALIA, WA 98531 • **1-800-206-9009**

WOODWORKING SURVEY

We always appreciate when people take time to write and let us know what they like and what they'd like to see more of. We know more of you would like to do the same, but find it hard to find the time. So here's an opportunity to do just that! It's easy - just grab a pen and mark a box! We'll personally look at every survey returned and use your responses to help design future patterns and projects.

1. My skill level is:

☐ Beginner   ☐ Intermediate   ☐ Advanced

2. I like to complete projects that are:

☐ Simple   ☐ Intermediate   ☐ Intricate

3. I prefer projects that require:

☐ Thin material   ☐ Thick material (3/4" or more)
☐ Both

4. I feel the amount of instructions/directions pertaining to the patterns/projects in this book are:

☐ Clear and sufficient
☐ Unclear and incomplete

5. My favorite pattern themes are: (mark all that apply)

☐ Wildlife   ☐ Religious
☐ Country   ☐ Floral
☐ Victorian   ☐ Sports
☐ Southwest   ☐ Holiday/Celebration
☐ Children's   ☐ Other _____

6. I would like more of the following projects:

(mark all that apply)

☐ Clocks   ☐ Baskets
☐ Shelves   ☐ Mirrors/Picture Frames
☐ Doll Furniture ☐ Plaques
☐ Birdhouses   ☐ Other_____

119

Fold here second

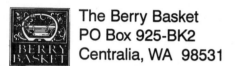
The Berry Basket
PO Box 925-BK2
Centralia, WA 98531

Place
stamp
here

The Berry Basket
PO Box 925-BK2
Centralia, WA 98531

Fold here first

COLLAPSIBLE BASKET PATTERNS
Over 100 Designs for the Bandsaw or Scrollsaw
by Rick and Karen Longabaugh

Collapsible Basket Patterns-Over 100 Designs for the Band Saw or Scroll Saw

By Rick & Karen Longabaugh

Making beautiful products is simple when you follow the five-step techniques described inside these pages.
• More than 100 different designs
• Easily made with a band or scroll saw
• Step-by-step instructions

$12.95

126 pages, 8.5x11, soft cover
ISBN# 1-56523-087-6

GENERAL SCROLL SAW

Become a Scroll Saw master!

All you taking advantage of your scroll saw? Most scrollers use only 10% of their saw's potential, but you can do more! The pattern and technique books on this page help to show you how to use your saw to achieve new results. From baskets to 3D miniatures, you'll discover hundreds of creative and beautiful projects for your scroll saw.

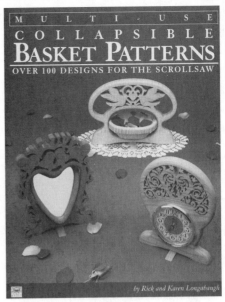

Multi-use Collapsible Basket Patterns-Over 100 Designs for the Scroll Saw

By Rick & Karen Longabaugh

Utilize the full potential of your scroll saw and in a few hours you can create beautiful projects in wood.
• 18 all-new designs (no repeats from book #1)
• Easy-to-follow instructions
• Create clocks, baskets, frames & more

$12.95

118 pages, 8.5x11, soft cover
ISBN# 1-56523-088-4

300 Christian & Inspirational PATTERNS
FOR SCROLL SAW WOODWORKING
BY TOM ZIEG

300 Christian and Inspirational Patterns for Scroll Saw Woodworking

By Tom Zeig

Start making projects with a deeper meaning.
• More than 300 never-before-published designs
• History of Christian symbolism

$14.95

173 pages, 8x10, soft cover
ISBN# 1-56523-063-9

Christmas Scroll Saw
PATTERNS & DESIGNS

Christmas Scroll Saw Patterns & Designs

By Tom Zieg

The extensive collection captures the warmth of the season. Some scroll saw knowledge required.
• More than 100 ready-to-use patterns
• How-To photos

$12.95

153 pages, 8x10, soft cover
ISBN# 1-56523-09

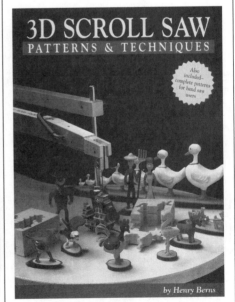

3D SCROLL SAW
PATTERNS & TECHNIQUES
by Henry Berns

3D Scroll Saw Patterns & Techniques

By Henry Berns

Gain a new perspective on your miniature work.
• Almost 50 3D projects for animals & people
• Explanation of 3D pattern techniques
• Band saw pattern section

$12.95

92 pages, 8.5x11, soft cover
ISBN# 1-56523-090-6

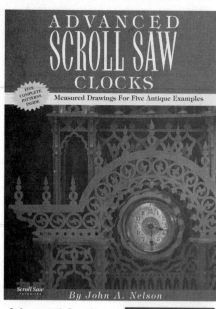

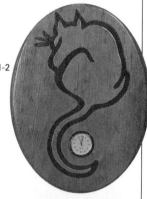

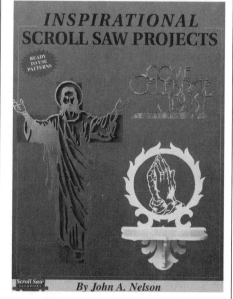

Scroll Saw Workbook

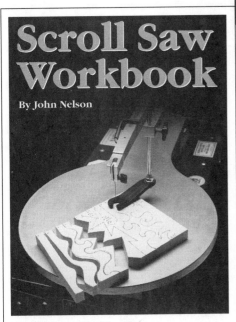

By John Nelson

Scroll Saw Workbook
By John Nelson
Draw upon John's extensive knowledge to learn every thing you need to know about
• Patterns included
• Fully illustrated
• Easy to understand
$14.95
96 pages, 8.5x11, soft cover
ISBN# 1-56523-117-1

JOHN NELSON

Catching up with the Nelsons

If you happen to meet John and his wife Joyce at one of the many shows they attend throughout the year, you'll be likely to hear about the latest scroll saw tip or technique. As a retired industrial arts teacher, John's first book was a teaching manual on drafting and mechanical drawing. Since combining his love for antique clocks, furniture and wooden projects with his aptitude for writing he has authored more than 40 books. His "Favorite Patterns" series of books includes patterns reproduced from the best of his design files.

Scroll Saw BASKETWEAVE PROJECTS

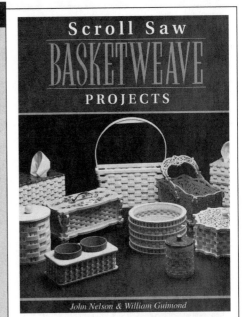

John Nelson & William Guimond

Scroll Saw Basketweave Projects
By John Nelson & William Guimond
Fool your friends with these intriguing baskets!
• 12 never-before-published projects
• Step-by-step instructions
• No special tools required!
$9.95
62 pages, 8.5x11, soft cover
ISBN# 1-56523-103-1

Making Wooden Baskets ON YOUR Scroll Saw

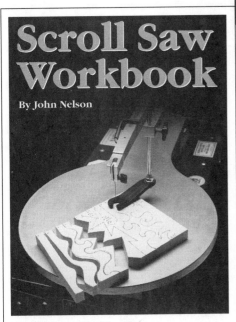

by John Nelson and William Guimond

Making Wooden Baskets on Your Scroll Saw
By John Nelson & William Guimond
Create beautiful baskets that could pass as hand-woven!
• Step-by-step instructions on cutting the "layers" of a basket
• 12 patterns including round, market, & square baskets & a tissue box
$9.95
60 pages, 8.5x11, soft cover
ISBN# 1-56523-099-X

---

3 Easy Ways To Order!

1 Order by Phone:
1-800-457-9112
or 717-560-4703
We are ready to assist you Monday - Friday 9:00 AM-5:00 PM (EST) Please have your Visa, Mastercard or Discover account-number ready. Voice Mail is available 24 hours a day.

2 Order by Fax:
717-560-4702
Just complete this order form or write your order on a piece of paper & fax it to us anytime!

3 Order by Mail:
Send your completed order form to:
Fox Books
1970 Broad Street
East Petersburg, PA 17520

visit our website www.scrollsawer.com

Don't Forget:
• Make all checks/money orders payable to: Fox Chapel Publishing.
• PA residents please add 6% sales tax.

For easy ordering outside the US, please use a credit card or obtain a US FUNDS money order at any bank or post office.

Shipping
Most orders are shipped within 24 hours. If you need your books right away, please ask about overnight service when you call.

Order Subtotal	Shipping Cost	
	USA	CANADA
$30 and under	$3	$5
$30.01 to $75	$4	$6
Over $75	$5	$8
FOREIGN orders will be billed the actual shipping cost.		

Meet Judy Gale Roberts

Raised by supportive parents in an artistic environment, Judy Gale Roberts had no problems deciding the direction of her career. Choosing an apprenticeship with her father over a formal art school education, she started working with many different media before focusing on wood. In the mid-1980s, she met and began working with Jerry Booher, a general machinist and toolmaker. Combining his mechanical ability with her artistic skills, they quickly developed a successful partnership. To this day they are still dedicated to increasing the knowledge and popularity of intarsia-artistry in wood.

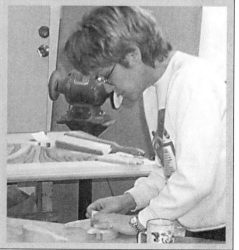